W9-BPG-323

UNDERSTANDING AND PREVENTING SUICIDE

UNDERSTANDING AND PREVENTING SUICIDE

The Development of Self-Destructive Patterns and Ways to Alter Them

Kristine Bertini

PRAEGER

Westport, Connecticut
London

Library of Congress Cataloging-in-Publication Data

Bertini, Kristine, 1955–
  Understanding and preventing suicide : the development
of self-destructive patterns and ways to alter them / Kristine Bertini.
      p. cm.
  Includes bibliographical references and index.
  ISBN 978-0-313-35530-1 (alk. paper)
  1. Suicide. 2. Suicidal behavior. 3. Suicide—Prevention. I. Title.
  HV6545.B428   2009
  362.28—dc22   2008046768

British Library Cataloguing in Publication Data is available.

Copyright © 2009 by Kristine Bertini

All rights reserved. No portion of this book may be
reproduced, by any process or technique, without the
express written consent of the publisher.

Library of Congress Catalog Card Number: 2008046768
ISBN: 978-0-313-35530-1

First published in 2009

Praeger Publishers, 88 Post Road West, Westport, CT 06881
An imprint of Greenwood Publishing Group, Inc.
www.praeger.com

Printed in the United States of America

The paper used in this book complies with the
Permanent Paper Standard issued by the National
Information Standards Organization (Z39.48-1984).

10 9 8 7 6 5 4 3 2 1

For my mother, Louise Carmen Bertini, who has instilled in me a ferocious life instinct and a great joy for living.

Contents

Acknowledgments

I am deeply indebted to all the patients who I have worked with over the years who have shared their joys and pains with me. This book would not have been written without the underlying context of those relationships, each of them rich and important. I have merged many of their stories in the case illustrations, always changing identifying information to maintain confidentiality. I am also indebted to those who have shared their stories specifically for this book. In these cases, I have kept the stories pure and changed only identifying information to protect the anonymity of the individual.

I especially thank those who have been my greatest supports: my husband, who has tolerated my absences, celebrated my successes, and grieved my losses; my parents, brother, and stepdaughters who support me unconditionally and are my greatest fans; and my friends who give me sustenance.

Included in my cheering section is the dear boss that I consider my friend, my esteemed clinical supervisor, my colleagues and team mates, and my technical advisors. You are all brilliant forces who promote good and right in the universe.

I salute and thank you all.

Introduction

The Maine potato is a hearty vegetable. Many Maine farmers leave their potatoes in dark burlap sacks in root cellars while they harvest. When a pinpoint of light emerges through a broken or dirty window in the cellar, the potato will seek this brightness with all its might. The potato's eye will find the light filtered by the sun and attempt to grow upward toward life.

In an inner city with sidewalks that are crusted over by layers of pavement and cement a sprout of grass will find its way up through a dry crack in the ground. This lone blade of grass will go unnoticed by the daily crowds of people who tramp over it. Yet it reaches up, like a small flag to the heavens, only to be trodden upon again and again. It is determined to have its moment in the light.

In small, dank ponds across the planet tiny amoebic creatures survive by feeding off the decaying substances that fall to the bottom of the pond. Without conscious thought, these creatures automatically seek survival. When the rains dwindle and the pond evaporates, these tiny, nearly invisible creatures seek other moisture to maintain their existence.

Life, even at the most primitive level, seeks to replenish itself and survive. In some of the most devastating circumstances and horrific conditions the human spirit fights to stay alive. Stories of individuals who have survived concentration camps, war crimes, family abuse, and near-fatal accidents give us evidence of just how strong the human spirit can be under the most catastrophic of circumstances.

This instinctual fight for life that permeates most people's existence can make it difficult to understand why some individuals want to die and, in fact, take their own lives by suicide. Unfortunately, suicide is not an uncommon phenomenon. In the United States, a suicide attempt is made every 18 minutes, and suicide claims the lives of 30,000 people each year.[1]

This book is meant to provide a full-spectrum view of suicide and recovery for both suicidal people and survivors of suicide. To create a better understanding of the suicidal mind, the factors that can lead to self-destructive acts are examined. Some of the first seeds for suicidal thoughts may be planted as the fetus develops in the womb. These early seeds of suicidal predisposition may provide clues to why people kill themselves.

The investigation into the suicidal mind is not a simple one. The path to completed suicide is complex and generally has multiple causes, which culminate in one final act of desperation. Each individual who completes suicide has his own unique trajectory that leads him down this path to self-inflicted death.

Seeds for an individual's suicidal predisposition may be planted early in the infant's development. However, other factors also can act as interventions to the development of suicidal intent. While this book will examine specific vulnerabilities to suicide and why some individuals may be predisposed to suicidal intent, it will also focus on the resiliencies that can be fortified or built within the suicidal person. These important human strengths are identified and emphasized in models for recovery for the suicidal individual. Resiliency is a key factor in suicide intervention, and a basic recovery program for the suicidal person includes personalized coping and resiliency-building skills. A clear and specific model of recovery for the suicidal individual is included in this book, which specifies methods for accessing help and a plan for positive action. Once a recovery plan can be put in place, imminent self-harm is reduced as supports are increased. There is hope for the suicidal person; this hope needs to be highlighted and understood. Predisposition for suicide is not a fatal diagnosis for completed suicide. Many individuals who have had suicidal thoughts do survive and lead healthy lives, even though they may have one or several of the risk factors that can lead to death by suicide. This book provides information and hope for suicidal individuals who may not realize that they have options other than to continue living a life that is filled with pain and despondency. Specific skills and coping strategies are provided that can assist the suicidal person in moving from despair to a desire to live.

In the tragic situation in which an individual completes suicide, survivors are left behind. Loved ones, friends, and colleagues are left to make sense of what may appear to be a meaningless act. Each of the 30,000 completed suicides in the United States every year touches at least six other people in profound and life-altering ways.[2] The impact of a loved one's suicide on family members, friends, co-workers, and acquaintances creates ripples of aftershock that may run deeply and last for years in those who experience the loss. Those who are left behind grieve; they try to understand and make meaning of the suicide, but often there is no complete closure or satisfactory answer to the question "why?" While there may not be concrete, clear answers as to why someone commits suicide, clues certainly can help those left behind to find peace. Included in this book is information for friends, family members, and co-workers who survive a loved one's suicide. The impact of the suicide, expected symptoms, and help for recovery for the survivor are discussed.

A fresh model designed specifically for the professional who is working with a patient who completes suicide is presented in this book for the first time. When a caregiver loses a patient to suicide, she experiences her own unique set of personal and professional responses. Little attention has been given to the professional survivor of suicide, and the model in this book offers one method that can assist the caregiver in her own recovery from the death of a patient. The caregiver may question her professional identity while she grieves the loss of her patient, and her response to suicide is unique and complicated. The model offered in chapter 6 proposes a guide to assist the caregiver in her own recovery.

Beyond the information and strategies that are provided in *Understanding and Preventing Suicide*, an underlying and, at times, direct theme throughout the book explores how humankind makes meaning of life and death. This meaning comes from cultural factors, environment, genetics, experiences, and a variety of sources that combine to make each person unique. It may be challenging to look at another individual and to comprehend how he made his decisions. It is particularly hard to understand when a loved one has made the decision to end his own life. Family members, friends, and all those affected by the suicide of a loved one must find some way to make meaning of the loss.

The final chapter in *Understanding and Preventing Suicide* attempts to navigate the existential components of suicide and ponders difficult questions, such as the right to choose death by suicide. Clearly, those who complete suicide want to die in the moment that they take their lives. Is this their fundamental human right? Why do others react so strongly if someone has taken her own life? Reactions to death by suicide and the meaning that surrounds this kind of death may result from primitive fears and projections of our own deaths. The moral, spiritual, legal, and ethical questions about suicide do not come with easy answers but are explored in this book.

The topic of suicide is profound and exposes some of the biggest questions and fears that we have regarding life and death. The materials in this book reflect the serious nature of the subject, but it is hoped that the theme of resiliency will shine through the pages and help the reader to find words of hope, comfort, and healing. The human spirit has the intrinsic ability and tools to seek life with greater resolve than the Maine potato, a sprout of grass, or a tiny amoeba. The desire to live is instinctual, and when pain and suffering can be diminished, the life force fortifies, magnifies, and blossoms.

This book provides a map of how the suicidal mind can develop. More important, however, a map of recovery is presented for the individual who may be thinking about taking her own life. When the force of life is beaten or worn down by internal or environmental factors, this book can become a resource to find new hope and a plan for replenishment of the battered soul. Stories in this book will provide insight into recovery and resiliency from individuals who were once suicidal and who have come back from the edge of death and are finding joy in their daily lives. Because some people will still choose the path of suicide, the words in this book may also provide some solace for those left behind and help them to make meaning of their loss.

Salute! To life and death, as it best suits each of us, and may we find comfort in each other.

1 ▪ ▪ ▪

Attachment: The Earliest Months and Years

The little one sleeps in its cradle,
I lift the gauze and look a long time, and silently brush away flies
With my hand ...

Walt Whitman, "Song of Myself"

▪ Case Example: Fragile Beginnings

The pregnant woman sat on the bench outside the shelter and rubbed her hands together to keep warm in the morning chill. She had just had breakfast at the shelter, and her stomach was full, bursting with the baby and with her morning meal. Her bags of belongings were at her side, and she sat planning her day. Two acquaintances from the shelter joined her, and they seemed oblivious to her pensive mood. She knew that she was due to have her child within the week, and she was feeling deep despair.

She had been homeless for at least a year; it was difficult for her to keep track of time on the street, and she could barely recall her life when she had had a roof over her head and her own bed to sleep in at night. Her days were now spent wandering, and her nights were in one shelter or another, depending on where she ended up at the end of the day or where there were shelter openings. She hadn't minded the shelter lifestyle until she had become pregnant. The baby's father could have been any number of men who also roamed the streets; the warm comfort of another body and the money she would get from the men had been enticement to have sex often. She planned to give the child up for adoption; she knew that she couldn't care for an infant on the streets.

She had many friends, and the people who lived the street life formed a kind of supportive family. They would sit in parks in the city and talk about each other, shelter staff, the best shelter food, and where to find whatever they needed. The shelter women who were not addicted to drugs or alcohol were particularly supportive of each other. She had tried to stop drinking when she found out she was pregnant, but there were some days and nights she just wanted to disappear, and the only way she could make that happen was to drink herself into oblivion. The next day she always felt shame and regret. She was aware that alcohol consumption could harm the baby.

When she thought of the time in her life before she had begun living on the streets, the memories were not pleasant. She had been raised in a home in which her father had physically abused her mother and brother; she had escaped the physical abuse by being her father's sexual object. She had left home as soon as she could and moved in with her high school boyfriend, who soon had become physically abusive to her. She had worked for a time at the local convenience store, but she began to drink heavily and fight all the time with her boyfriend. Then she had lost her job for continually arriving late. The abuse from her boyfriend had become worse, and one night she had left their apartment and stayed at the local shelter. Shelters and the streets soon became her new home.

At first, life on the streets had been preferable to the existence she had been living with her family and then her boyfriend. She was free to come and go, could always have a hot meal that she didn't have to cook, had other women around her who liked to drink, and had a place to sleep. She could easily get money for alcohol from men who wanted sex. She had felt free and, at times, even powerful. However, when the weather had turned colder, she had had her doubts about street life for the first time. She had not liked being cold, and she had started to feel depressed. There were times that the shelter staff had to prod her out of her cot in the morning, and she had found that she was crying all the time, both when she was drunk and when she was sober. When she had realized she was pregnant, she had had thoughts of suicide but had not had the energy or means to kill herself. The shelter social worker had helped her to get well-baby care and arranged to give up her child for adoption. She didn't really care about giving up her baby; her maternal instincts were either deeply buried or had been killed off by her father when she was a child. The only feelings she was experiencing toward the baby inside her were guilt and shame when she drank. She knew from the well-baby clinics she sometimes attended that alcohol poisoning could affect her child's growth.

She felt the first labor pains that day, and as she walked to the hospital, they became worse. Her labor was fast and furious, as though the child wanted to be born quickly and to get away from her as fast as it could. She never saw her child and did not know if she had had a boy or girl. She was relieved to have the baby out of her body, so she would not have to feel guilt anymore. She could believe that the child was in a better place, with two parents who could care for the baby better than she could. She would recover from her labor, she thought, and go back out to the streets and finally decide what she wanted to do with her life.

The infant, kicking and screaming in a fit of rage, was taken from her birth mother and placed in the hands of a middle-class woman waiting expectantly with her husband in the next room in the hospital. They had rushed to the hospital when they had heard the baby was coming; this was the moment they had dreamed about for years. The baby looked perfect, soft, and healthy. Her squawks were endearing to the new parents. The child's fingers and toes were tiny and sweet; its small features were endearing. They had her name picked out and finally could take their own child home to its freshly painted bedroom and new baby things.

These new and adoring parents took their beautiful infant home. They were aware that the child's mother was a street person. They assumed that since the child had never had contact with its mother after birth, she would not have any influence on the baby. They did not completely understand the role that heredity, genetics, and the unconscious can play out in a child's life.

The first few weeks were full of excitement and newness for the couple. They were happy to be up at night with the infant, who was colicky and did not sleep well. This was what they had been waiting for all these years. They had good patience and used all the techniques they had been taught in their parenting classes and books. They loved to show off the infant to their family and friends and to just sit holding the child, even though she was high strung.

The infant seemed to have an angry temperament and did not soothe easily, no matter how much the new mother rocked her. As the first weeks grew into months and the child still did not comfort easily, the parents did not understand. They believed that if they were consistent in their care, rocked the child endlessly, changed and bathed and fed the child with love, the infant would settle into a peaceful routine. When this did not happen, the new parents began to experience frustration with the colicky and temperamental child. Their patience abated as the infant continued to scream through the night, and sometimes they would leave her to cry for long periods of time. It seemed that the longer she was left in the crib, the harder she would cry. Yet if they tried to rock her, she would ball up her fists and arch her back in anger.

As the stress with the child continued, the parents began to find themselves arguing and fighting more between themselves. The arguments were loud, and the child would wail in the background as if she were mimicking her parents.

This infant, born to an alcoholic street woman who had experienced periods of depression, clearly exhibited predisposition for issues with temperament. This type of challenging temperament of the infant, unfortunately, created frustration for the baby's primary caregivers, who subtly pulled away from her as all their attempts to soothe her failed. Additionally, the home became a battleground as her parents experienced stress and took it out on each other. The child's heredity also created vulnerability for her in the possibility of transmitted genetic alcoholism and depression. A cycle of frustration, failed attempts at soothing, and further frustration by both parents and child became enacted. As the parents pulled away, the child began to feel neglected. If this pattern continued into early childhood, the seeds for environmental depression could compound the genetic susceptibility obtained from her birth mother. This child became at risk for suicidal predisposition and alcoholism.

In home environments in which biological or environmental predisposition for depression exist early, interventions are the best means to alter or diminish the future impact of negative functioning. For example, one useful intervention for this infant could include child care relief for the parents. Providing new parents with consistent breaks from a challenging infant or young child can give them the time they need to decrease stress and spend positive time with each other. As they experience time away, they will feel more able to be present with the child. The child will unconsciously feel the decreased stress in the parents and will soothe more easily. Additionally, as the parents spend positive time together, they will argue less, and the child will not hear the sounds of anger and violence in the home that accompany parental discord. A second intervention for the colicky and temperamental infant and child is the development of a positive, loving relationship with a supportive other. This supportive other could be a grandparent, aunt, or paid caregiver. The benefits of having a supportive other can be life altering for a temperamental child. This caring other may be the one person who can provide unconditional love or acceptance, even if it is in short amounts of time. It can be easier for the supportive other to provide this unconditional esteem as such a person is present for shorter periods of time and, therefore, will not become as frustrated with the child. Additional resources that can help new parents include parenting classes to assist with understanding differences in children's temperaments and support groups in which parents can express their stress and parenting strategies.

■ Three Scenarios

An infant cries. Its parent reaches into the bureau drawer and pulls the child out and close to the chest, the heart. Soothing, cooing love sounds from the adult radiate through the child. Gentle and tender touches and rocking motions lull the infant into an altered state of reverie. Love is transmitted from the parent to the child with every movement, touch, and sound. The infant gurgles and safely nestles into the crook of a sheltering arm.

Another infant cries. Its parent is distracted and impatient with the sound. Feeling disturbed and interrupted, this parent reaches for the infant. The parent's touch is not gentle. The infant arches its back and responds with louder cries. The adult bounces the infant in an up-and-down motion in the hope that the crying will stop, but the child wails all the more loudly. The parent feels frustration at the infant's continuous needs, and the bouncing becomes more pronounced. The infant unconsciously picks up the parent's resentment and reacts with its own rage until it cries itself into a fitful, sweating sleep.

A third infant awakes in its crib. Its cries are unheard. It is not picked up or held. It is wet, and hungry. Its fists shake in rage and unknown terror. The parent is sleeping, or away, or in a drug-induced state. The infant wails, and in time hands reach into the crib and pick up the child. These hands are not the parent's hands. They belong to another adult and seek to quiet the sounds of the child. The parent responds only intermittently and with ambivalence, and the infant is left to the devices of the world.

■ In Utero

In a mere instant in time, a seed melts into an egg, and a baby is conceived in a womb. The fates determine much of how and where this infant will begin its life and what the internal and external conditions that affect the womb will be as the fetus develops. The baby's parents may be wealthy or poor; they may reside in a third-world country or in an urban, metropolitan city. The child may be born in perfect health or with any number of medical issues. The infant's parents may have been awaiting the birth of their child with joy and excitement, or the parents may be despairing that their child is being brought into the world.

These fates begin to affect the infant even before the child is born. In its mother's uterus, the fetus senses its environment and the world around it through the shallow depths of the stomach lining. According to Ellenor Mittendorfer-Rutz and others, good mothering begins well before the day of birth.[1]

A pregnant woman may shelter the child growing in her womb from the world's harshness by limiting her contact with loud sounds, violent people, and images that disturb her own emotions. This mother may be a woman of privilege who has the financial, physical, and emotional resources to surround herself with loving others, good nutrition, and calming music. The fetus is honored and cherished, and the mother cares for her body, so the child will grow in a womb protected from negative outside forces. As this mother limits her own stress, her fetus grows in an environment that is stable and unmarked by trauma. This fetus unconsciously begins to sense the world as a loving and consistent place.

In contrast, another mother may live in a world that is laced with turmoil. There may be violent others in this woman's environment who affect her emotional health and feelings of well-being. The fetus can feel the vibrations of this mother's stress, and negative electrical charges will penetrate the tiny cells that are forming. Some mothers may not have the resources to provide proper nutrition for the growing fetus, and this too can affect the development of the growing child. Drinking alcohol, smoking cigarettes, and using substances can also affect the fetus, because "[i]ntrauterine and postnatal environment together have crucial and equally important roles ... and early stressors contribute to the likelihood of later suicidal behavior through an interaction between genes and environment."[2] Other influences, such as the parent's biology and heredity, may affect the growing fetus. Medical issues that can affect later functioning in the world may begin in the early formation of the cells as they are transmitted from one generation to another, from parent to forming child. The groundwork for genetically transmitted physical imperfections such as multiple sclerosis, cancer, and Alzheimer's is laid in the first months of life. Other biologically carried seeds from the parents may be planted for later mental health issues such as depression, attention deficit disorder, and anxiety.

Environmental and biological parenting factors in the early development of the fetus may seem formidable and can be the precursor for
later issues in life. They are important to note, as they, indeed, play a
role in the character of the infant. In chapter 3, the individual's resiliencies and vulnerabilities are detailed, and these qualities can be seen
to alter the course of biology and the environment in an individual's
life. Fate has its moment in the creation of the fetus and child; self-
determination of the individual also will be seen to have its place.

Attachment

The early attachment of the infant to its caregivers can create the foundation for all relationships to come in the child's life. Donald Winnicott
described the infant's environment as being a critical factor in the
healthy development of the child. He believed that, when the environment is good enough, it can foster the maturational processes of the
infant. Winnicott used the term "good enough mother" to describe the
parental role of providing sufficiently for the child to get a good start in
life. He believed that when the parent is successful at meeting the infant's
gestures and needs, the child's development will include genuine, happy,
and spontaneous behaviors.[3] Winnicott also believed that if the environment is not safe, the individual builds up a false set of relationships.[4]

Most theorists conclude that early attachment patterns of the infant
and child influence later relationship patterns. The infant that is held,
caressed, and revered by its significant others develops a sense of secu-
rity and an unconscious knowing that it will be cared for, fed, and
comforted. These early sensations are the foundation upon which the
child can create a strong and healthy sense of self. Caregivers who have
the internal and external resources to provide a consistently nurturing
environment for the child foster independence, self-esteem, and harmony in the developing person.

In contrast, Winnicott stated, "Failure of the environment to adapt
to the needs of the child can lead to interference with the normal
growth processes that lead to the establishment of a self that goes on
being, achieves a comfortable harmony with the body, and develops a
capacity for relating to others."[5] If repeated failures in child care occur,
the development of the individual may not be true, spontaneous, genuine, or integrated. The child may develop into an adult with various
kinds of neuroses.[6]

It is satisfying to think about the child that is born into a family of
good emotional resources. The caregivers are able to provide the child
with emotional comfort that is necessary to design a healthy internal

world; this child is held and supported through all the travails that he will face and learns just how to navigate the planet under the watchful eye of his parent. This youngster will be taught the skills to master the emotional challenges that life throws at him. This child will grow into an adult who can adapt to change and to the inevitable life hardships that are bound to confront him. Although this person may be surrounded by some early difficulties such as poverty or a biological illness, he will also have learned through good parenting that he can master and survive these difficulties.

The world has many barriers to developing a healthy sense of self. However, when an infant grows up in a home that is supportive and loving, a foundation is created in which the developing self will flourish, even under adversity. The toddler who is praised and rewarded for good behavior will begin to cement the knowledge within herself that she is lovable and worthy. Her self-esteem will be built first from the outside in; as she is provided with positive reinforcement, she eventually will come to believe that she is, indeed, a treasure to the world. This internalization of self-worth will fortify the child through challenging times, building further resiliency as she masters life's difficulties.

In comparison, the infant or developing child who does not have loving and consistent parenting faces the world at a great disadvantage. Sigmund Freud wrote that anxiety in children is nothing other than an expression of the fact that they are feeling the loss of affection from the person they love. He went on to parallel this with his hypothesis regarding neurotic anxiety in adults. Freud stated that the core of anxiety is a repetition of the affect experienced at birth and in the early years.[7] Christopher Tennant stated that situations in which the child does not have his needs met due to the emotional unavailability of the caregiver are great contributors to adult psychopathology, particularly depression. Tennant's research indicates that parental deprivation of the child contributes to the individual's emotional difficulties in adulthood.[8] John Bowlby reported that states of anxiety and depression that occur during adult years can be linked systematically to states of anxiety and depression that occurred between child and caregiver. Bowlby stated,

> [W]hereas during later life it is often extremely difficult to trace how a person's disturbed emotional state is related to his experiences, whether they be those of his current life or those of his past, during the years of childhood the relationship between emotional state and current or recent experience is often crystal clear. In these troubled states of early childhood can be discerned the prototype of many a pathological condition in later years.[9]

Imagine the child who is left to master his environment without consistent love and support. This child's basic needs of food and shelter may be satisfied, but her need for parental affection and consistent parenting is absent. In some cases, the child is reared not only in an environment of passive neglect, but also one in which emotional or physical abuse may be present. This child may be subject to a resentful and angry parent, from which a foundation of fear and anxiety is created. The growing person may witness rage that is manifested in a loved one being battered by another, or the child may experience physical harm herself. How can this child develop a healthy sense of self? What does this child learn about the world and others in it?

The first task of the child who is raised in an environment that is unsafe is to survive. Children learn quickly that, if a caregiver is violent, they can avoid harm. These methods of avoidance come at great cost to the developing self. Spontaneity and genuine wants and feelings must be pushed below the surface and a pretend self created. This pretend self becomes a complex combination of accommodation or resistance to the adult's needs, and an underlying development of significant rage or depression can begin. As the child grows its protective accommodation or resistance strategies become more sophisticated and the genuine self is buried more deeply. These accommodations are extremely functional during childhood as they serve to keep the child safe from the parent's wrath. As the child becomes an adult, however, the old defensive patterns are no longer functional and affect the sense of self, well-being, and relationships with others.

Compounding environmental stressors that affect a child's development include any hereditary factors that have been transmitted from the parent or that developed uniquely in the growing youngster. These factors could include physical impairments such as hearing loss, bone structure deficits, speech difficulties, or a variety of other issues. Medical challenges experienced by the child also can significantly affect the relationship between parent and child. The adult may come to find the many necessary hospital trips and doctor's appointments a frustration, and, thus, the child may come to feel like a burden to the family. If the parent is unable to provide the medically compromised child with supportive care and understanding, this child can experience distress that results not only from the illness, but also from the lack of compassion from the loved one.

Children who inherit mental health issues from their parents, such as depression, anxiety, attention deficit disorder, bipolar disorder, autism, and, in later years, substance dependence, also experience a disadvantage if they do not have a parent who is understanding and responsive to the specific nature of the illness. These issues may become exaggerated when the loved ones react with anger, distaste, or even hostility to behaviors that result from the child's mental illness. Instead of helping the child to learn to manage his symptoms and flourish, the parent who misunderstands mental health issues may instead further push the child into a deeper state of disruption.

The early caregiver's reactions to the physical and mental health issues of the child can create long-term responses from the child that can affect her feelings about self and others in later adulthood. The dynamics that are set in place in early infancy and childhood are powerful legacies that profoundly affect the adult. For example, a child who has been born with a debilitating illness, such as cerebral palsy, has already begun her existence at a disadvantage. If this child is also born into an environment that has limited physical and emotional resources, she will be in true psychic jeopardy. The child's parents may be overwhelmed with the cost of medical appointments. They may be unaware of the unique psychological needs of this child, or they may be caught in their own dysfunctional cycle and unaware of the attention that a special-needs child requires. Long-term health issues that begin in infancy or childhood can place a burden on a family, and if the caregivers are not vigilant, their resentments may be transmitted to the child. Not only does this developing young self have to master her own medical challenges, but she begins to internalize the fact that she is a burden to her loved ones.

Among the many factors that influence the development of the child are the cultural, religious, and social allegiances the family has formed. These factors may be multigenerational and contribute to the image the family has created for itself and instills into the new family member. For example, being born into a family that is part of an underrepresented ethnic group has its own unique compilation of responses that affect how the child may greet the world around him. If this family has been treated with bigotry and hatred, it is likely that the child will pick up wariness, anger, and mistrust from his parents. The sense of the child's self will be affected by how the world has responded to his family's not being a part of the privileged majority. The same can be said for a child who is born to poverty, or to a religion that is not part of the mainstream culture. Difference can breed fear and prejudice, and cultural factors can be the focus of hate crimes from others who are full of ignorance and rage. At very young ages children can instinctually understand when they are not revered. While a child may not understand the reasons for bigotry, feelings of rejection can be internalized and create significant issues with self and others.

Some family cultural attributes may be more visible than those of other cultures. A child born into an African-American family is black, and the color of her skin tells the world her ethnicity. An Iranian child also will look different from the mainstream white culture in the United States, and her difference could propel a bigoted person to act in hatred. A person of Russian descent, however, may appear to be from the mainstream white culture and therefore may not experience acts of discrimination because she appears to be similar.

On the other hand, if a child is born into a cultural group that is part of the privileged majority or mainstreamed culture, he may feel more accepted simply as a result of his culture. These children will not have to manage prejudice inflicted by fear of difference. They can more easily settle into their homogenous communities and never even have to consider what it might be like to be a person of difference.

The cultural norms of the family can have a significant impact on the child. Cultural norms are adopted by family systems and are often unspoken ways in which the family interacts and relates to the outside world. Some family norms are invisible, such as being born into a family that is stoic in nature and does not express feelings or ask for assistance from others in their community. Cultural values such as these can be transmitted nonverbally, and the child who is raised in a stoic environment may learn by witnessing others in the home that her family does not show vulnerability. This child may hold feelings in and isolate herself. The cultural norms of an African-American family may also be invisible to the outside eye. This family may face bigotry as a result of its African-American culture and difference in appearance, which is visible; they may also have invisible differences, such as religious beliefs that are not held by the mainstream. The child born into this family may experience both the multigenerational pain of African-American oppression and the present impact of religious difference.

The child makes meaning in his world through his own experiences and by watching his caregivers interact with him and others in his environment. Each caregiver comes with his own history and culture, his own positive and negative dealings with the world. As the child witnesses the adult interact with others around him, the child begins to make his own meaning from these interactions. The growing person may begin to see the world as a good and safe place if that is what the parent believes and how the parent interacts. Or, if the parent is fearful of others, the child may begin to interpret the outside world as a dangerous place.

Carl Jung wrote about the collective unconscious and described how images, thoughts, feelings, and behaviors can be transmitted for generations between groups, families, and individuals. Jung stated that the unconscious exerts a formative influence on the psyche that we may ignore consciously but respond to unconsciously. He described this part of the psyche as retaining and transmitting the psychological in-heritance of mankind.[10]

According to Jung's theory of the collective unconscious, a child born into a family that has descended from tragedy many generations ago may pick up and carry the unresolved grief or rage from decades past. This child may not be aware of where or how the sadness origi-nated, but it could be an underlying emotion to the formation of the self, transmitted through the generations.

The impact of the collective unconscious is a fascinating twist to the child's development. Fate, environment, heredity, culture, and the past all combine to design a child's formation. In the remainder of this chapter, the early development of suicidal tendencies will be tied to each of these factors. In chapter 2, the subsequent impact on adult-hood will be detailed.

■ The Seeds of Suicide

And as to you Life I reckon you are the leavings of many deaths,
(no doubt I have died myself ten thousand times before).

Walt Whitman

It would seem to be simple common sense that a child who experiences a warm and loving childhood will grow into a secure and well-adapted adult. Many children do grow to be healthy and functional members of society. Even in the healthiest of homes, however, children may experi-ence moments when their parents are not available or are distracted or even neglectful. In those homes that do develop a positive sense of self in the child, the moments of caring and love far outnumber the moments of parenting failures. Every parent will have many moments of distraction and emotional unavailability to the child. When a parent has an illness or is facing a challenge at work or experiences a serious life event, it is obvious that this parent will not be entirely attentive to the child. That inattention will be short lived, however, and the overall attachment of parent to child will be positive and attuned.

Conversely, it is not rocket science to predict that a child raised in an environment lacking empathy and consistency may experience later life problems. The extent of these later life problems may be deter-mined by the levels of ambivalence, antipathy, neglect, or abuse experi-enced by the child. Children are dependent on their parents from the moment they are born. They arrive into the world somewhat a blank slate, and they learn from their environment and the people who are closest to them. If they have caregivers who are not loving and consistent with them, they will have a core foundation that is not secure and is vulnerable to life's many challenges.

In a significant study by Barbara M. Richards, she concludes that in the view of psychotherapists, more than half the patients who have attempted or succeeded in completing suicide have experienced rejection and abandonment in their early years. Parents were often perceived as absent and unavailable, and a high percentage of the patients reported feeling disconnected from their mother and father. These individuals developed a bleak, impoverished inner world, which contributes to suicidal thoughts, feelings, and actions.[11]

In a home with unavailable, emotionally neglectful caregivers, the child is left to her own devices, and the internal development of the self is based on impressions the child can gather in this void. The lack of mirroring of the self leaves the child to design her own vision of who she is in the world. Because the craving for love and support is so great and yet so unattainable from the neglectful caregiver, the child begins to formulate a sense of self that is empty and forlorn. The child may come to believe she does not deserve her parents' love and affection, and the harder she attempts to earn this love, the more her self-esteem is eroded. As this negative cycle of seeking love and being rejected repeats itself, the feelings of negative self-worth solidify. These feelings may not necessarily be conscious in the early years; however, this is the period in which emotional memories are hard-wired in the developing brain. The negative beliefs about self and others are formed and cemented in the child's neurons. Neglect of the child leads to the child's feeling unlovable, and this emotion can be carried by the child into adulthood. Low self-worth, depression, and anxiety become a foundation for both the child and the developing adult's relationships with self and others.

Powerful feelings of low self-worth and depression can lead to thoughts of death and suicide, both in childhood and in adulthood. Indeed, depression is one of the leading symptoms of the suicidal person. Overt suicidality may not develop in the child until later years; however, many young people who have unrecognized, untreated depression can experience suicidal thoughts and feelings. Some children may even attempt to take their own lives. These suicide attempts often go unrecognized by the adults around them. The attempts may be disguised in the form of what can appear to be accidents. For example, a young child who consciously puts himself in the path of a moving car or truck may be mistaken for having done so by accident. Children may seek to escape pain and abuse at home in many ways. They may use strategies of compliance, avoidance, or more dramatic gestures of self-destruction. Some of these self- destructive acts may not be intended to cause death; rather, they may be a matter of caring so little that the child's risk-taking becomes dangerous, even lethal. Other examples of these types of behaviors include jumping off bridges into water, using substances, playing dangerously close to machinery, riding a bicycle at high speeds in dangerous traffic, and even playing with unattended weapons left in the home. Self-destructive acts by children may be impulsive and can be either conscious or acted on without conscious thought.

One study found that childhood emotional abuse created a deep longing for closeness and fear of rejection that leads to an inability to develop basic trust and "accounts for the relation between childhood emotional abuse and suicide attempts in adulthood." Heather Twomey and others go on to note that emotional neglect can be even more devastating to the development of a healthy self than the more overt forms of physical or sexual abuse and that ultimately this neglect may lead to suicidality in adulthood.[12] The effects of emotional neglect can be insidious and have long-term consequences. Emotional neglect is more difficult to identify than physical abuse, and, therefore, it often goes unrecognized and untreated.

In taking this discussion of a child's development one step further, the child who is physically, verbally, or sexually abused faces numerous challenges. John Briere and Marsha Runtz note that individuals who have attempted suicide report higher levels of childhood sexual and physical abuse than others who are demographically similar.[13]

Physical and sexual abuses are appalling ways in which some children are greeted by the world around them. Both types of abuse are extraordinary boundary violations that inflict fear, pain, and suffering on a developing self, sometimes by a most trusted loved one. The impact of being a victim or a witness to these kinds of violence creates a profound wounding of the psyche. The young child has few emotional resources with which to make sense of what is happening to him; he only knows that he is not safe. Physical abuse has many faces and can be inflicted routinely or haphazardly. Some physical abuse occurs when a caregiver is intoxicated and for no particular perceived offense; other physical abuse may be suffered routinely as the child is trying to learn to navigate his surroundings. Physical abuse is not about the child or because of the child; it is a result of rage and disturbed power issues within the adult or older perpetrator. Unfortunately, the child receiving the abuse does not understand this and takes in the belief that he deserves the pain.

Children who are sexually abused have their own complex set of responses and symptoms. These children become the "object" of an older person's power over them. The perpetrator may use his or her power to intimidate, terrorize, and bend the child to his or her own will. The child feels she must comply or she will be destroyed in some fashion. Compounding the confusion of the sexual abuse is the biological fact that at times the act of sexual touch can feel good to the child. The immature mind does not know how to make sense of the pleasure she feels when she also is aware that she is being violated and used.

A child who lives in fear of being beaten or sexually abused develops a strong sense of mistrust and a self that must be compliant to the needs of the other. The true self becomes sacrificed, and a false persona is developed so that the child may survive. Underlying the false persona grows anxiety, depression, and rage. The child may be so affected and feel so isolated and alone that he begins to experience a wish for death to escape the confusion, fear, and pain. Unconscious suicidal behaviors may begin during this time, and some of the signs may be seen in the form of dark artwork, risk-taking behaviors on the playground, and impulsive acts that lead to further punishment. Conscious suicidal thoughts and behaviors can also begin at an early age. Some children will tell a teacher that they "don't want to be around" anymore or may begin self-cutting behaviors. Other children will spend their time drawing pictures of heaven and become preoccupied with death, asking many questions about what it is like to die and how it might feel to be dead.

It is clear that there is true cause and effect between the early treatment of the child and the environment in which she is raised and the development of suicidal tendencies. When a child is raised in a home with love and responsiveness, low self-worth and suicidal thoughts are less likely to develop than in a home with neglect or verbal, physical, or emotional abuse or multiples of these factors.

Heredity can play a significant role in an individual's development of suicidal thoughts and behaviors. As discussed earlier in this chapter, biological seeds begin to be transmitted from parent to child in utero. Genes for mental health issues such as schizophrenia, bipolar disease, depression, and suicidality can be passed through the generations, along with the color of the infant's eyes, the shape of the child's face and body, and other physical attributes. Thomas Joiner states, "[s]uicidal behaviors run in families, and this fact has to do with genetics and neurobiology as well as genetically conferred personality traits."[14] Genetics creates a part of the foundation upon which the individual will develop; the environment adds to this foundation and can have either a positive or negative influence on the biology of the child. Family studies give evidence of the role of genetics in those who attempt or complete suicide, and twin and adoption studies clearly show that genes are involved in suicidal behavior.

Brain chemistry also may have an effect on a child's predisposition for depression and suicidality. Serotonin is a neurotransmitter in the brain that regulates mood and emotion. Low levels of serotonin can cause depression and potentially lead to suicidality. A single gene, located on chromosome 17, is responsible for encoding the serotonin transporter gene. If this gene is compromised, low levels of serotonin can result. When these faulty genes are passed through familial bloodlines, low levels of serotonin will be shared from generation to generation, parent to child. Family biology and heredity can be responsible for a disadvantaged transporter and subsequent low levels of serotonin. Low levels of this substance in the brain alone, or compounded by a poor environment, can affect the positive development of the self. Feelings of low self-worth that are generated in the home by the caregiver will be more difficult for the individual to overcome without the necessary level of serotonin to keep mood stable.

Cultural factors and the collective unconscious may influence the developing self and suicidal tendencies. In some ethnic groups, the numbers of completed suicides run much higher than in other ethnic groups; this may be a result of genetics, environment, learned patterns within the group, or the impact of the privileged culture on the smaller, underprivileged culture.

Consider the child who is raised in a village in the developing world in which several of the adolescent males and young men have completed suicide. In some developing countries the village is like a large family and any loss affects each member of the group. The male child raised in this village unconsciously carries knowledge that suicide is a familiar way in which families have lost their sons to death throughout the history of their people. In this culture, a deep and long-standing sadness may be unspoken and carried by each village member. As the Western world affects this culture, developing acculturation issues, as well as alcoholism, may compound the feelings of loss and lead to further suicides in the village. An example of this type of culture can be found in the Pacific Islands. The rate of suicide for young men in these islands is astronomically high. As the generations in this culture pass, depression and suicidal predisposition are transmitted from one family member to the next through genes and cultural norms. Many young boys may have lost an older brother or uncle to suicide. As these boys reach the teenage years and are faced with alcoholism and the impact of Western culture, their sense of self is in doubt. They have witnessed their older family members die by suicide. They witness their cultural ways of life being affected by industrialism but may have no means to join the new culture without feeling they are abandoning or disrespecting the older cultural traditions. The Western world has introduced alcohol, and their systems react to the substance as if it were poison. They quickly become addicted. When intoxicated, they become self-destructive and often complete suicide. The village mourns their youth. These young lives are lost to unconscious ghosts of long ago.[15]

In the smaller urban nuclear family, there may also be a long history from generations past of completed suicide. Stories of a great-great-grandfather who shot and killed himself may be passed down from mother to child. This same family may also include an aunt or uncle who took his or her own life, or a series of family members who have died by suicide. In some families and cultures, the completed suicide(s) may not be discussed; however, the feelings of loss can be passed unconsciously through the years. One family member's suicide may be the precursor to another's suicide many years later. Similar to depression and other forms of mental illness, alcoholism can be passed down generations of cultures and families. When alcohol is used by an individual who is already depressed, it can create a deadly combination for death by suicide. Suicide attempts, suicide gestures, and completed suicides often occur when a depressed person is intoxicated. For individuals with poor impulse control, the use of alcohol or drugs lowers inhibitions and may propel the person to act without much forethought. When an intoxicated person who has thoughts of self-harm also has the means handy to kill herself, the risk is great for completed suicide. Substances may provide the individual who has had thoughts of suicide the false bravado to actually act on her intent. Even when these individual reach out for help, it can be difficult for those who may wish to intervene to stop the deadly course of events.

Genetic mental illness, substance abuse, culture, and environmental factors all contribute to the development of the self. It is clear that the infant and developing child have little control regarding the state of matters in their early lives. Some lucky children may be born and raised in a family in which the gene structure is not laced with mental illness or addiction and the home environment is warm, loving, and privileged. However, other children begin at a disadvantage by inheriting defective genes from their biological parents and by being raised in a home or culture with many emotional challenges to overcome. Some children are born into familial or ethnic cultures with long multigenerational histories of suicidal behaviors; some are not. The child is not responsible for the family or culture he is born into or the biology he inherits. However, he must somehow find or be presented with the resources to function with what he is given. The following chapter will discuss how the early formation of trends toward suicide in childhood can affect the adult. Chapter 3 will address the way these individual can survive and flourish, even with beginnings that are laced with multiple challenges of biology, environment, and culture. Many adults have been able to take their adversities and use them to their advantage. The travails of the child raised with the challenges of a compromised family hereditary, neglectful or abusive caregivers, or a culture composed of multigenerational suicides can be overcome. The resiliency of the human spirit is remarkable, and with courage and fortitude many obstacles can be mastered and redefined.

Many interventions can be useful in assisting a child who may begin life with genetic or environment challenges. It is especially important that adults be aware that each developing soul needs to be considered special and cherished. Caregivers may not be aware how much power they have in molding the life of a child and the lasting impact that their intervention can have in later years.

The following are early signs of suicidal tendencies to watch for in childhood:

- Crying often
- Moodiness or extreme emotionality
- Isolation
- Being overly quiet
- Not eating or overeating
- Drawing dark, sad, or violent pictures
- Trouble sleeping
- Talking about death
- Talking about "not wanting to be here"
- Wishing to be in heaven
- Acting out, showing aggression
- Impulsivity or dangerous acts, such as playing with fire or running into traffic
- Lack of play or spontaneity

Caregivers can thwart the development of suicidal tendencies in infancy and early childhood by demonstrating the following behaviors:

- Creating a loving and nurturing environment for the infant and child
- Eating and sleeping well; ensuring the child eats and sleeps well
- Limiting the use of substances
- Touching the infant and child often and with love
- Playing with the child
- Listening
- Creating consistency in routines
- Limiting stress in the environment

- Playing soothing music
- Laughing
- Showing affection
- Asking the child what she worries about and listening carefully; showing care and concern for the child's concerns
- Providing positive responses to behaviors
- Limiting negative responses
- Removing harmful toys and creating an adult "watch" if there are concerns that the child may harm himself with impulsive behaviors
- Letting the child know that the caregiver is there to help
- Spending extra time with the child
- Taking the child seriously and not ignoring words or behaviors that are warning signals (listed above)
- Taking the child to a professional counselor if the behaviors persist
- Seeking counseling if feeling overwhelmed or if there are questions about what should be done for the child

▓ Eliza's Story

Eliza is a nine-year-old girl, from a white middle-class family, who is brought to see a therapist by her mother, Bethany. Bethany reports to the therapist that Eliza has been coloring pictures of heaven and saying she would like to be "up there" with her puppy. Eliza's dog was hit by a car and killed several weeks earlier, and her mother explained to Eliza that the dog had gone to heaven. Before the puppy died, it had been the focus of Eliza's world. The puppy had slept with Eliza at night and followed her about the house during the day when Eliza was home from school.

In gathering a family history the therapist learns Eliza is a quiet child with few friends. Eliza is described as spending a lot of her time alone in her room drawing. Eliza's mother reports that she and her husband separated the previous year. Prior to the separation, there had been a lot of arguing in the home, and Bethany admits that both parents drank too much alcohol. Eliza's father had left the house after an especially bad argument and had not returned. Eliza has not talked much about her father moving out, even though Bethany has asked repeatedly how Eliza feels. Since the separation, Eliza's father has been visiting her once a month on Saturday mornings.

Eliza's mother reports that Eliza is eating and sleeping well and that she has not seen Eliza crying, even when the dog was killed. To Bethany's knowledge, there is no family history of depression or suicidality in her own family or in her ex-husband's family. Bethany states that she started to become worried about Eliza soon after the puppy had been killed and Eliza had asked many questions about heaven and what it is like there. Eliza had also asked Bethany if she would go to heaven if she got run over like her puppy. Soon her drawings had taken on similar images of sky and light and a puppy and a girl on a cloud. Eliza had told Bethany that she was the girl in the picture. Eliza's father thinks that Bethany is making too much of Eliza's pictures and statements. Bethany, however, tells the counselor that she is alarmed because Eliza seems to be preoccupied with heaven and even wants to be there with her dog.

Several risk factors can lead one to conclude that intervention would be helpful for Eliza. She obviously is preoccupied with the loss of her puppy and with thoughts of death and heaven. Eliza's mother is astute enough to realize that Eliza needs help and to take her daughter seriously when she says that she would like to be in heaven with her puppy.

Eliza's behaviors include the following risk signs for depression and suicidal predisposition:

- Desire to be in heaven
- Pictures of herself in heaven
- Isolation
- Lack of friends
- Parental separation
- Loss of contact with her father
- Limited interaction with her mother/family
- Loss of beloved pet
- Possible low self-esteem
- Arguments between parents
- Substance abuse of parents

Eliza exhibits significant risk factors for depression. She is isolated and has little social contact with friends her age, which is a developmental milestone for her age range. It appears that she has no close playmates either at school or at home. This social isolation may affect her self-esteem as other children around her surely are involved in activities that are age-appropriate. Compounding the social isolation, Eliza comes from a home in which there has been turmoil between her parents and then the sudden loss of the intact family system. It seems that there had been little discussion or explanation for Eliza when her father left home. Her contact with him decreased immediately and became limited. Eliza then experienced the loss of her beloved pet, perhaps the one contact for her that had always been loving and consistent. There is some question of substance abuse by Eliza's parents, which could affect their ability to develop strong attachments to Eliza. Additionally, Eliza's father minimizes her symptoms. In her way, Eliza appears to be telling a story through her pictures of how she wants to die and be in heaven with her puppy.

The good news in this family is that Eliza's mother is taking both her daughter's verbal and nonverbal cries for help seriously. Bethany had become concerned and called a professional when Eliza had stated that she wanted to be in heaven with her puppy. In response to concerns like these, the counselor could provide an evaluation for Eliza to determine levels of depression and safety. The therapist would also design a treatment plan to assist Eliza and her family in identifying and implementing methods of recovery. Several therapeutic strategies could be utilized to help Eliza feel better about herself and her life. First, the therapist would engage Eliza and help her to begin to verbally express some of the angst she was feeling. Eliza's art could act as a catalyst for this communication. The therapist would also engage Eliza's father in the treatment and help him to see that his daughter is, indeed, experiencing feelings of deep sadness and loss. Ideally, increased visitation would be arranged between father and daughter, and Bethany's one-on-one time with Eliza also would be increased. The therapist would teach Eliza coping strategies and social skills while working with her parents to improve their parenting skills. The counselor could provide resources for parenting classes of divorced couples and education regarding substance abuse and its impact on the family. Overall, Bethany's intervention of bringing Eliza to counseling could have a dramatic positive effect on Eliza and the family system.

The following methods of repair are recommended:

- Begin talk and play counseling for Eliza with a professional
- Increase consistent weekly visits with father
- Increase positive time and interactions with mother
- Increase positive reinforcement from parents (to improve sense of self)
- Increase social time with peers (play dates)
- Consider same-age counseling group participation
- Limit arguments between parents, especially in front of Eliza
- Create awareness in parents of substance abuse its impact on Eliza
- Attend parenting classes for divorced couples

In her play therapy with her counselor, Eliza draws a picture of her family, which includes only her mother and herself. In the picture she draws herself very small in a corner. Her mother takes up most of the picture and is distant on the page from Eliza. Eliza's therapist is able to use the picture to help Eliza talk about her loneliness and fear. She does not understand why her father is gone from the home, and she misses him greatly. Eliza also has great fears that her mother will die. The therapist helps Eliza put words to her fears and facilitates direct communication between Eliza and her mother. Eliza's father is invited to a session with Eliza and her mother, and together they talk about the divorce and what it means to Eliza. Eliza's father also sets up more visitation time each week to spend with her.

While Eliza may not have been imminently suicidal, she certainly exhibited symptoms of depression. Without treatment Eliza's symptoms could have increased in severity, and eventually she may have become actively involved in gestures of self-harm or suicide. The process of becoming suicidal could have developed slowly or happened more quickly. In some cases with similar symptoms, the depression does not develop into active suicidal intent. When a young child exhibits serious signs of depression that include talking about wanting to be in heaven (death), it is important to pursue an evaluation with a professional. Early intervention by Eliza's mother was instrumental in a number of ways. First, the fact that Bethany took notice and sought professional help provided Eliza with evidence that her mother cares about her and loves her. Second, Eliza was able, with the counselor's help, to put her sadness and fears into words and express them, rather than keeping them internalized. Third, the family dynamics were altered by the therapist's recommendation that both father and mother spend more consistent quality time with Eliza. Eliza was able to experience her needs being met in a reparative manner.

■ Conclusion

The seeds for predisposition to suicidal tendencies may begin even in the womb. Genetics, environment, culture, temperament, and fate all play a part in creating both vulnerabilities and resiliencies in the infant and child. Each vulnerability factor, or a combination of factors, may put the developing person at a disadvantage for well-being, both in the present and in later years as an adult. The earlier that an intervention can occur the better. If mental health issues can be identified at an early age, skills can be developed within the family to help with change and adaptation. Then, in later life, some learned skills will be in place to manage the challenges that life presents. Without early intervention, the problematic issues can continue to grow and fester; they may combine with new issues relating to the environment and the developmental stage of the individual. The following chapter contains a detailed discussion of how vulnerabilities and risk factors in early childhood may affect the functioning of the adult. Chapter 3 will explore how vulnerabilities for risk to suicide can be mitigated by resiliency factors. It is imperative to understand that although a child may have a number of risk factors that could predispose her to suicidal intent, a multitude of resiliency factors can offset these vulnerabilities. With help, understanding, and intervention, suicidal action can be averted. There is hope.

2 ▪ ▪ ▪

The Legacy: Life Responses

... the house is narrow, the place is bleak
Where, outside wind and rain combine ... with a malice ...
O enemy sly and serpentine.
Do I hold the past
Thus firm and fast
Yet doubt if the future hold I can?

Robert Browning

▪ Case Example: A Learned Response

Rebecca had good insight. She could see that she was in yet another abusive relationship, and that she had fallen into a familiar pattern. All the men on the planet could not possibly be so cold and hard. She wondered if she was a magnet for men who didn't want a caring, long-term relationship. The men she had been involved with seemed to use her, take advantage of her kindness and then leave her. Some of them were verbally abusive. One of them frightened her half to death when he threw a lamp at her wall and then threatened to hit her with it.

Most of them moved into her life, stayed a short while, and then had their affairs and moved on, leaving her behind.

Rebecca had hoped that her last relationship, with Jim, would last forever. Jim seemed to be conservative and solid, and Rebecca thought he was someone who would want to settle down. He was divorced with two young children. Rebecca thought they were like abandoned kittens that needed her care and love. She cooked their meals at night, rearranged her small home so that they could live comfortably, and stocked her refrigerator with Jim's favorite foods. She did their laundry, shopped for their groceries, and had Jim's two finger gin and tonic waiting for him every night when he came through the door from work. Jim did not offer to help Rebecca pay her mortgage and utilities or assist with the grocery bill. Rebecca did not bring up the subject of finances because she was fearful that if she did Jim would leave. Her girlfriends asked her if Jim was sharing the household bills and she would lie to them because she was embarrassed.

Jim would come home at the same time every evening, sit with his gin in the living room, and pull the newspaper in front of his face. Then he would watch the news while Rebecca made sure the kids were bathed and had finished their homework. She would cook dinner and clean up. Jim would go to bed every night promptly at nine o'clock. Rebecca liked the fact that she could count on Jim's schedule and that she could tell others that she was in a relationship. She did feel badly that he did not take her out much, or bring her flowers. Jim also did not introduce her to his colleagues at work. This began to make her feel insecure, and she tried to find ways to go to his office so that she could meet the people that he knew.

After eight months had passed Rebecca began to hope that Jim would talk about their future together and perhaps about becoming engaged. She wanted to know that someone would love her and always be there for her.

When Jim left her, she hit her bottom. He had met another woman at work and although he would not admit that was his reason he was leaving her, Rebecca knew. Rebecca and Jim had lived together for almost a year and she was heartbroken and simply wanted to die. She didn't want to live alone anymore; she felt unlovable and worthless. She could barely force herself to get up in the morning to go to work, and she stopped eating. She fantasized about walking in front of traffic.

One night, she picked up the telephone book and looked under counselors. She knew she was in crisis and had to do something so she started to make calls. She left many messages on therapist's answering machines and several of them did not even call her back. The counselors that Rebecca spoke to were booked and not taking new patients. One or two of the counselors spoke with her at some length and were kind and gave her referrals to call. Rebecca couldn't believe that she couldn't even find a counselor willing to meet with her. Finally, a male therapist called her back and was able to fit her into his schedule. When she walked into his office for the first time Rebecca couldn't stop crying. She couldn't talk. She just cried. The therapist was patient and sat with her and scheduled another appointment with her for that same week.

Through her therapy, Rebecca came to understand that she had been raised in a home in which her father was preoccupied with his business. He traveled often and was seldom at the dinner table. He never attended Rebecca's important childhood events. Looking back, Rebecca could almost feel the indifference that emanated from her father; until she began counseling she had not realized that her father suffered from clinical depression and had trouble engaging with his children any more than superficially. Rebecca's mother was kind and full of laughter; however, she was preoccupied with her own friends and enjoying her own life. Rebecca came to realize that as a child she felt like she could never ask for anything from her parents. She went along pretending that her life was fine even when she suffered from little girl hurts and teenage needs. Rebecca had teenage acne, which made her feel self conscious and shy; she just never felt good enough for others and found herself spending a lot of her time reading books and in her room daydreaming. Rebecca could recall one poignant snapshot from her teenage years that seemed to capture her feelings of aloneness. She had gone to a New Years Eve party a few blocks from her house and as it neared midnight all her friends had partnered off with boys except Rebecca. She felt awkward and uncomfortable, and knew that she would not be missed by her friends, so she walked the few blocks home. Her parents were having a party themselves. It was freezing cold outside, but Rebecca could not bring herself to walk into the house to the questions her parents would ask about her being home early. She sat on the snow-covered, icy steps and watched the adults count down to midnight through the window. They all seemed so happy and it was clear they felt that they belonged. Rebecca felt lost, alone, and out of place. She waited another 20 minutes in the cold and then tried to sneak past her parent's company to her own room upstairs.

When Rebecca was 18, she felt actively suicidal for the first time. In her earlier years she had often pondered the meaning of life and death, and there were many times that she wished she would just not wake up. This time, however, Rebecca sat in her parent's kitchen and used a steak knife to make sharp cuts on her arm. She wondered what drugs she could take from the medicine cabinet that would kill her. One of her friends called and interrupted her actions. Rebecca never made any other active gestures of self harm in the following years, but often wondered about the reason for her living.

During her therapy, Rebecca came to learn that she had a distorted belief system that had been created during her childhood. In part, the belief system was unconscious, but became played out in her adult life. Rebecca's primary caregivers did not have the time or attention for her, so that as a young child Rebecca came to believe that she must be unlovable. She thought that if she was quiet and "good" and took care of others that her parents would love her better. She thought that if she just did more around the house and did not complain, someone would finally notice her and provide her with the love and attention that she craved. As Rebecca grew up and entered adulthood she played out this scenario again and again in her friendships and with men. She would give herself fully in her relationships and not ask for anything in return. When others would not respond to her or left her she would always ask herself, "what's wrong with me?" Despondency would then set in as Rebecca felt the hopelessness of being alone.

Rebecca's insight from her therapy helped her to see that her patterns of giving more and more of herself did not work. Her relationship with Jim provided Rebecca with the clear evidence that the more she gave the less he appreciated her and the more she felt helpless. Although Rebecca could not see it at the time, Jim's abandonment provided her with an opportunity to look deeply at her core patterns and make changes that could lead her to healthier, more fulfilling relationships. As Rebecca learned not to give so much of herself away and to ask for what she needed, her relationships became more satisfying. While Rebecca had insight and could see the ineffective patterns she had engaged in, they were difficult to change. It took time, practice, and work in her therapy to overcome her old ways of reacting. Evidence of positive outcomes when Rebecca would have small successes helped her to continue to slowly change. She felt more hopeful, less helpless, and over time Rebecca established a sturdy relationship with a partner who shared life's challenges. Years later, when she looked back at her relationship with Jim, Rebecca could directly relate her choices to her early childhood.

■ Core Patterns

The early years in the life of each individual set the foundation for the formation of the adult self. As the child grows, her home environment sets a mold, and the adult steps out of this molded cast and into the world. This chapter discusses many of the life responses of the adult who has been raised in a home where a cast has been set for suicidal tendencies. The symptoms and behaviors of the suicidal adult are complex and designed from the unique factors of the individual's upbringing, heredity, and internal constitution. There is not one simple pattern but a constellation of issues that can be identified. Each individual makes meaning of her own existence in a manner that is her own, and the following pages are meant only to provide illustration of some of the many ways that the adult may translate her pain into a self-destructive act. It is hoped that if some of the signs and symptoms of adult suicidality can be recognized in their earliest forms, completed suicide can be averted by interventions that are addressed in chapter 4.

Chapter 1 explored the early causes and the development of suicidal tendencies in the child. This chapter discusses the effects of these causes and several of the salient individual factors that foster adult suicidality. The chapter concludes with a discussion of how these factors, alone or in combination, can be deadly, as well as interventions that can avert suicide.

■ Internalized Despondency, Learned Helplessness, and Rage

The combination of internalized despondency, learned helplessness, and rage, or any one of these factors alone, can create a miserable existence for any human being. These feelings contribute to low self-worth, lack of pleasure in life, depression, hopelessness, and destructiveness. They limit the abilities of the healthy adult and can create significant impairment in daily functioning. Individuals experiencing long-standing despondency, feelings of helplessness, or rage have relationships with significant others that can be affected dramatically in adverse ways. These individuals do not have the emotional energy to create and maintain levels of intimacy that are needed for a healthy adult relationship, or they use what energy they have to act out in destructive ways. Therefore, they may often find themselves isolated or in a relationship that is unrewarding or abusive. They may become victims, believing that this is all the world has in store for them. At work, the despondent, helpless, or vengeful individual may not reach his potential or fulfill his basic responsibilities. His colleagues and supervisors may develop disdain for his continued inability to function fully or his disruption of the workplace. Many times an inverted cycle of negative responses is created in which the despondency, helplessness, or rage leads to failure. This failure then manifests into greater despondency, helplessness, and anger, once again proving to the individual that he is, indeed, worthless.

■ Despondency

Internalized despondency is a deep-seated belief that there is no hope or help in the world; it is one of a constellation of symptoms that, if left untreated, can eventually lead an individual to clinical depression. A despondent adult who has come to have a core belief that there is little hope of positive experiences plods through life finding little joy or pleasure even in small things.

The despondent person may feel as if she has sandbags attached to each foot; each movement and action can take an incredible amount of effort. Sleep and appetite may be disrupted, and thoughts may cycle in a negative vortex in the despondent person's mind. Sadness may accompany the despondency; anger may be present, but the energy to fulfill angry fantasies generally is not available to the person who is despondent.

In some cases, despondency may be the beginning of clinical depression; in other cases, despondency may be one of a constellation of symptoms that are the result of an existing biologically induced depression. In yet other cases, despondency may be environmentally carried from childhood or a reaction to an unresolved life tragedy.

When despondency is the result of biological factors that lead to clinical depression, there can be symptoms such as sleep disturbance, appetite changes, ruminating thoughts, and loss of interest in pleasurable activities. The despondency that leads to a depressive episode may be triggered by a traumatic event, such as the loss of a loved one, a car accident, or any other tragic circumstance. Biological despondency and subsequent clinical depression may surface without an environmental cause. As the length of time that an individual experiences her symptom(s) increases and does not receive treatment, the despondency and depression can deepen.

Despondency that is carried from childhood may be a pervasive part of an adult individual's personality. This despondency may have been the way that the child survived a difficult childhood; that is, by shutting down and minimizing reactions to his home environment. It could also have been a learned emotion from caregiver's responses to the world. The child has learned to mimic the adult and unconsciously seeks the same attention or secondary gains his parent received from being maudlin. These learned traits can be difficult to identify and alter in later life as they have been mechanisms that the individual uses to function and feel safe in his early years.

Despondency alone or in a cluster of other symptoms that result in clinical depression can lead to suicidal thoughts and behaviors. Living under a dark cloud for a long period of time diminishes the ability to believe that life can have pleasure. Negative thoughts and low self-worth may drive the wish for life to end. Edwin Shneidman said, "[p]sychological pain is the basic ingredient of suicide. Suicide is never born out of exaltation or joy; it is a child of the negative emotions."[1] The individuals for whom a primary feeling is despondency simply want to end the psychological pain they are experiencing. Suicide may present them with the only option they can see; it may be a means to feel some control over a destiny that otherwise looms ahead as large and black. The despondent person often can see no other way out of the pain she is experiencing. If she has carried the heavy load of sadness and pain for many years, death may appear to be an oasis of peace and calm, beckoning like water in the desert. For the person who is experiencing overwhelming sadness from the loss of a loved one or a recent traumatic event, death may appear to be the only way for her to resolve her hurt. She is unable to see clearly through the deep pain of loss to find other options or a glimmer of hope. These individuals want only to stop the hurt, and the only way they can see to end their pain often is to end their own lives.

While despondency may be created by deeply ingrained beliefs about the self, these beliefs can be altered. The cognitions that make up negative beliefs and thoughts can be worked with and changed. The negative thoughts that are embedded in an individual's psyche may be tenacious; however, once they are recognized, they can be identified each time they occur. And once the thoughts are identified, they can be replaced with positive self-talk. The process of changing deeply ingrained beliefs requires time and hard work. Imagine the mind as a tape that has been set with a single set of negative messages that had been replayed again and again for years. Erasing the negative messages may be difficult because they are embedded in the rehearsed tape. With practice and repetition, however, the messages can be rewritten and new, hopeful messages can be engrained on the tape. Once a new set of positive messages are designed and become repetitive for the individual, they will slowly come to believe the new words. At times, the individual may fall back into the familiar negative ways of thinking, but over time, these events will become the exception rather than the rule.

▇ Helplessness

Learned helplessness, as its name indicates, is a feeling of powerlessness that originates from repeated attempts to gain mastery and control that fail. Learned helplessness is not a biological phenomenon, rather it comes from circumstances present in the environment. Continued feelings of helplessness may eventually join with a cluster of other symptoms to create a biologically engineered clinical depression. By itself, however, the feeling of helplessness originates from continued oppression in the environment.

Adults who have been raised in families who are from underrepresented populations may experience the feeling of learned helplessness. These individuals are not a part of the mainstream privileged white majority and can experience prejudice simply because of their skin color or nationality. These underrepresented adults have learned from an early age that they are different and at risk of violent behavior from others because they are not the same as the majority. Imagine an adult from a minority group standing at a bus stop with several people from the mainstream culture. This adult may experience fear, anxiety, and helplessness as they wonder if they may be confronted because they are different. The individuals from the mainstream population seldom have to worry about prejudice and generally are not aware that the person of difference has concerns for their well-being. The fears may arise from an experienced history of abuse or be reactive to the present situation. Regardless, the helplessness generated from being in a minority is real. Vigilance to the surroundings is felt to be necessary to remain safe from possible threat. Other persons of difference who may have experience oppression from the majority culture include those individuals with physical handicaps, those who look different, and those who live in poverty. Those belonging to the privileged majority continue along without awareness that the individual of difference is experiencing anxiety. This unawareness contributes to the underrepresented persons' feelings of invisibility, isolation, and fear.

Similar to those from underrepresented populations, a white child who is abused may feel helpless to stop the abuse in their environment; this abused child goes unseen and unheard as the adults around them betray them with violence. When abused children of any culture or nationality grow into adulthood these early feelings of helplessness can continue. For example, the adult may choose relationships in which his needs are not met and feel helpless to change the pattern. Oftentimes for these adults a repetitive life pattern exists in which they choose partners or employment in which they become victims of abusive others. The helpless individual may unconsciously reenact his early years in the hopes of mastering the past; however, without intervention the familiar dynamic of abuse takes over, and feelings of helplessness remain and grow. It is much like a moth to a flame. According to Roberta Satow, "Freud believed that repetition compulsion was an unconscious drive toward self-destruction and a reflection of the death instinct. Most psychoanalysts have rejected the concept of the death instinct and believe these repetitive behaviors were originally adaptive and necessary for the child's psychic survival, but in adulthood they are self-destructive."[2] This is not to say that the adult survivor of childhood abuse or the adult from an underrepresented population wants to feel helpless or abused; rather, old familiar patterns may unconsciously take over and life events become played out to match early experience.

Learned helplessness is a state, much like despondency, that can lead to suicidal thoughts and feelings. As the adult feels trapped in an abusive life cycle and can see no way out, suicide can provide him with a choice and a feeling of control. For the helpless individual, the thought of suicide may be not only for escape, but also may be viewed as a manner in which to "punish" the perpetrators or to gain the ultimate attention and power. This can be a magnetic fantasy; the helpless person may believe that he can finally have the last say. As the helpless adult feels more and more exhausted by his life of being a victim, he comes to understand that he can exert a lasting blow on the perceived "abusive others" by killing himself. The thought of this power becomes more and more seductive until the adult who feels helpless becomes moved to inflict self-harm.

The feelings of being helpless that have been created over time are not a fate that is locked into a person's personality. While there may be some effects of hard-wired patterns in the brain from early exposure to abuse, these patterns can still be altered. With the help of a therapist to identify patterns and implement change, the individual can move to more effective functioning in the world. A therapist can assist this person in identifying healthier relationships and a safer living environment. For the person from a minority culture the reality is that there may not always be safety in the environment. However, strategies and ways to navigate the world may be identified to make life less threatening.

■ Rage

Despondency and learned helplessness are reactions to life circumstances that become internalized by the individual. Rage is yet another reaction to negative life circumstances that develops internally but is manifested externally, either against the self or others. The child whose needs have been thwarted or who has been abused or ridiculed may develop into an adult with a grudge against the world. This adult's sense of self has been distorted through words and actions of early caregivers, and the reaction may be to strike back. This adult may seek to punish others through her own acts of abusive behaviors. As a child, this person was very likely unable to express any form of healthy anger for fear of punishment from the caregiver. The feelings of anger were suffocated, and the child was left to experience feelings of injustice and stifled, long-standing internalized rage. As this child moves into adulthood, the internalized rage may become safer to express and is externalized. This is extreme rage; the years of holding the anger inside have left the adult with no skills to modulate the intense emotion. The anger that spills out is generally disproportionate to the circumstance and frightening to the person receiving the furious reaction.

Externalized pervasive rage erodes the adult's relationships and, subsequently, any potential for positive self-regard. As the uncontrolled eruptions of anger destroy the adult's home life, work relationships, and friendships, this person may wallow in self-loathing. Samuel Vaknin said,

> The first layer of anger, the superficial anger, is directed at an identified target, the alleged cause of the eruption. The second layer, however, is anger directed at himself. The patient is angry at himself for being unable to vent off normal anger, normally. He feels like a miscreant. He hates himself."[3]

Anger can be the result of an abusive or neglectful early home environment. It can also be experienced by those from minority groups who have lived with oppression as a child or experienced violence or hatred as a result of their difference. Learned helplessness may translate into rage as the years unfold and the child becomes an adult.

As might be imagined, rage may be accompanied by a plethora of other emotive states. Self-loathing, self-pity, remorse, despondency, and jealousy complicate the enraged person's emotional state(s). Clinical depression may also be present, and suicidal or homicidal thoughts and actions may begin to take on a deeper role in the angry person's fantasies. This can be a dangerous person as the anger is often impulsive and, if it is present in combination with drug or alcohol use, the result may be lethal. Unfortunately, the world has witnessed many acts of violence in which a raging individual has killed others and then committed suicide. Some of these acts are premeditated, well thought out, and planned. Other times they happen in moments of impulsivity or intoxication. According to the Violence Policy Center, approximately 1,500 deaths in the United States occur each year as a result of murder-suicide. Murder-suicide is particularly tragic in that it generally involves more than two victims and may involve a family with children.[4]

Suicide may be the only option that the rage-filled person is able to see following an act of violence toward others. The latest episode of anger may have been one in a series from which he can finally see no other way out. Killing himself may be seen as the only way to stop the violence he perpetrates or the single action that can stop the feelings of shame he experiences.

The angry person may also feel that she can "punish" others by taking her own life. For example, if a romantic relationship or a position of employment has ended against the enraged person's wishes, she may decide to "show" the other person(s) what they have done and kill herself in an impulsive act of retribution. Similar to the despondent and helpless person, the rage-filled person may not realize that she has options other than suicide.

Rage is an emotion that is born from circumstance, entwined in events that include the actions of others and the reaction of the angry individual. While the actions of others may not be under control of the individual, the response of anger can be changed. The shift from rage to a healthier response takes insight, awareness, and a willingness to change. The individual who possesses these criteria for change can work with their support system and design a plan for addressing their anger. As the anger diminishes, a wealth of other feelings yet untapped are often found within the angry person, awaiting attention and release. As the process of attending to these other feelings and needs are addressed, the individual's rage diminishes and a healthier self arises from the wreckage. A part of healing for the angry individual may be to make amends for the hurt they have caused others with their reactions. The journey to making amends may take time, but marks the road to significant, healthy change.

▓ Distorted Belief System

The person who attempts suicide has developed a strong negative belief system that may include several components. These beliefs have been internalized from an early age and are a powerful force that consumes the adult's thoughts and behaviors and can lead to suicidal intent. Distorted beliefs are cognitions that can become embedded in a person's thoughts. When children are repeatedly told that they are bad, unattractive, and stupid or given any other negative message on a routine basis, they can internalize these messages. These internalized thoughts then become beliefs about the self.

Distorted beliefs of the suicidal adult can include the thoughts that she has no other option than suicide, she is powerless to stop the negative patterns in her life, and she will always feel despondent, helpless, or angry. These individuals may believe that they are a burden to others because of their negative impact on those closest to them. The belief that they cannot make changes and that their lives will be a continued cycle of the same miserable feelings propels them to want to end their days.

The suicidal person may harbor the belief that he has nothing to live for and that his days will continue on hopelessly, full of pain, and without any measure of joy or happiness. Because his significant relationships have been affected by his emotional state(s), this person may be isolated or surrounded by others who also have become weary of the distress he constantly experiences and projects. This isolation and rejection further affects the suicidal adult and solidifies for him that there is nothing left for him. He feels exhausted and overwhelmed, and he cannot believe that tomorrow may be different.

Unfortunately, the suicidal person also can have fantasies that her death will bring her sympathy or revenge. She may spend time imaging how the important others in her life will feel after she is dead. She may have the belief that her suicide will "teach" her family members, coworkers, and friends just how bad she was feeling or that suicide will show them how much she will be missed or how much she was misunderstood or mistreated. Her own funeral may be replayed in the suicidal person's mind with key players acting out the desired outcome of grief and anguish. This imagined drama provides some level of proof to the suicidal person that she is loved and will be longed for after she is gone.

Perhaps the most universal and destructive distorted belief of the suicidal person may be the belief that he is unlovable and that nothing can change this fact. These feelings of unworthiness may be a core belief that started at a very young age when he was not nurtured and revered as a child. In adulthood, when this individual experiences fractured relationships, he can feel many of the same emotions that he did as a child. The feelings of being unlovable subsequently grow and solidify. Even the smallest rejection by another may trigger earlier feelings of abandonment or abuse and add to the pile of evidence the adult is compiling to prove that he is, indeed, not worthy. The suicidal adult takes the belief that he is unlovable and creates a more self-destructive belief that he will *never be loved*. He cannot see his way out of this faulty assumption; therefore, the future looms large and bleak. Many mental health issues arise from the underlying core belief of the adult that he is unlovable. Issues such as depression, anxiety, adjustment reaction(s), self-mutilation, and other factors that develop in reaction to the environment and upbringing can have devastating long-standing effects that eventually may lead the individual to suicidality.

Just as the negative feelings that accompany despondency can be altered, distorted thinking also can be changed. It can at times be difficult to determine whether distorted, negative thoughts come first for some individuals or they begin with feelings of despondency that continue in a negative downward spiral. In some respects it is not so important to make this distinction. Rather, the importance falls in changing the thoughts so that the individual can come to understand and believe that they are lovable and worthwhile. Cognitive behavioral therapy can be most helpful in altering negative thoughts, and the therapeutic relationship can provide an environment in which the individual can feel likeable.

■ High-Risk Factors

Statistics show that several factors and multiple populations are at the highest risk for attempted or completed suicide. These factors and populations are noted below and are especially important in helping to recognize the suicidal adolescent or adult. Without knowledge of the signs to look for and the groups that may be most affected by suicidality, many suicidal individuals will not receive the help they need to avert death. Other factors and groups at high risk may not be listed below, but those that are listed are the most predominantly featured in the literature on suicide.

Following are the high-risk factors for suicide:

- Mood disorders, particularly depression
- Other mental health disorders
- Substance abuse
- Low self-worth
- History of previous suicide attempts and hospitalizations
- Impulsivity
- History of physical or sexual abuse and disruptive behavior
- History of deliberate self-harm
- Opportunity (that is, easy access to firearms, and so on)
- Family history of suicide and mental health issues
- Serious medical illness

The following populations are at high risk for suicide:

- Adolescents
- Runaways and the homeless
- The elderly
- White men—for completed suicide
- Women—for suicide attempts

- Gay, lesbian, transgender, and gender-questioning individuals
- Native Americans
- Native Alaskans
- Pacific Islanders

According to the U.S. Preventative Services Task Force (USPST), risk factors for attempted suicide are mood disorders, comorbid substance disorders, and a history of previous suicide attempts. Other risk factors that are noted include aggressive behavior and a history of physical or sexual abuse. The USPST reports that two-thirds of suicidal deaths occur on the first attempt, with higher completion rates for men than for women. Women may attempt suicide more often than men, but men use more lethal means and have a higher rate of success in killing themselves. More than 90 percent of the individuals who complete suicide are reported to have a psychiatric illness at the time of death, usually depression, alcoholism, or both. The USPST goes on to report that 75 percent of suicides are completed by white males. Caucasian males complete suicide twice as often as African-American males. Native Americans are also suggested to be at high risk for suicide.[5]

It is interesting to note that the most privileged group in society, the white male, has the highest rate of completed suicide. Marginalized groups such as the elderly, gays and lesbians, Native Americans, Pacific Islanders, and the homeless also are at high risk. Statistically, these marginalized groups have smaller populations; therefore, the numbers that are based on volume may not correctly represent proper analysis of the data.

Additionally, alcohol and drug use is noted to be highest among the more marginalized high-risk populations listed above, such as Native Americans, Native Alaskans, Pacific Islanders, and the homeless. The use of substances may place an already high-risk individual in an even more vulnerable position. Intoxication leads to distorted thinking, increases depressive states, and promotes impulsive behavior. The combination of substance use and existing suicidal intent or newly emerging suicidal thought may be disastrous.

Traumatic events may also be a precipitant to suicidal thought or action. Some of these events can include the issues of relationship difficulties, such as a recent breakup or divorce; financial difficulties; loss of employment; major losses caused by events, such as a tornado, fire, earthquake, terrorist attack, and so on. Any traumatic event that creates great distress can lead some people to feel that suicide is their only way out. Many of the warning signs for suicide are listed below, along with resources for the suicidal person and for the concerned other. These warning signs should be taken seriously and help should be sought from a professional. Suicidal thought and intent is treatable, and if help is obtained, many suicidal people go on to lead happy, healthy, and productive lives.

Following are the signs of suicidality in adulthood:

- Disturbed sleep
- Loss of appetite or overeating; sudden weight change
- Crying
- Loss of interest and pleasure in activities
- Missed work
- Increased substance use
- Impaired relationships
- Thoughts of suicide
- Talk of wanting to die
- Giving away treasured items
- Increased moodiness and anger
- Fatigue
- Difficulty concentrating
- Decrease in sexual drive
- Isolation
- Interest in wills and insurance policies
- Increased energy and improved mood just prior to suicide attempt

What to do if **you** are experiencing suicidal thoughts or feelings:

- Talk to someone:
  - Relative or friend
  - Therapist (see phone directory under "Counselors")
  - Spiritual or clergy leader
  - Health care provider
- Call the National Suicide Prevention Hotline (1-800-273-TALK) to speak to someone immediately
- **Understand that suicidal thoughts and feelings are symptoms that CAN be helped and changed if you reach out**
- Avoid additional stress:
  - Comfort yourself with favorite, relaxing things such as a cup of tea, a warm bath, talking with a friend, grooming your pet, reading a novel, or watching a light comedy
  - Take the pressure off yourself; don't set goals that may be hard to reach or put any additional responsibility on yourself
  - Surround yourself with people who are loving and supportive
  - Be gentle with yourself

What to do if you are concerned that **someone else** may be suicidal:

- Encourage the person to talk:
  - Listen
  - Ask questions
  - Let the person do most of the talking
  - Tell the person that things can change
- **Help the person make an appointment with a counselor and offer to accompany them to the visit if they wish**
- If possible, remove any method of harm, such as weapons, drugs, or alcohol
- Take the person seriously
- Don't be afraid to talk about suicide; talking about it will not make it happen

If the suicidal person refuses help, remember that help is available for concerned persons from a counselor. Concerned persons can call the National Suicide Prevention Hotline (1-800-273-TALK) to get names of counselors in the area and to get assistance from a hotline therapist about how to talk to the suicidal person. Concerned people should do not take on the role of counselor themselves or feel that they can be the one to "rescue" the suicidal person. A professional will know the best way to help. Individuals concerned about someone else being suicidal also need help themselves in dealing with this dangerous situation. Do not try to manage it all alone.

The life responses to early childhood discussed in this chapter that can affect the adult and lead to suicidal thought are all treatable with professional help. The combination of cognitive therapy and medication has an extremely high rate of success for these individuals. For suicidal people who are reluctant to take medication, counseling can have a positive effect by itself in many cases; for those who are adverse to "talk" therapy, medication alone may be successful. However, the highest rate of success is in individuals who combine counseling with medication.

Suicidality is a debilitating and complicated phenomenon with many faces, as shown in this chapter. It is tragic when a suicide is completed because the symptoms, with help, can be reduced and, in many cases, eliminated.

The following chapter will explore the individual's vulnerabilities and resiliencies in managing suicidal thoughts and feelings. A person may emerge into adulthood with many early predisposition factors for depression and suicide. The individual, however, may also have internal and external resources for changing his or her own destiny.

3 ▪ ▪ ▪

Vulnerabilities and Resiliencies

▪ Case Example: Making Lemonade from Lemons

Her digital music player was so loud that others could hear the music as she walked through the gym. She had her eyes half-closed and was imagining herself as the singer. She could see herself on the stage with her backup band and the thousands of fans in the audience screaming her name. She knew every word of the song by heart, and there were times she had to consciously stop herself from singing them out loud. She imagined herself making eye contact with one of the boys in the imaginary band who was playing guitar. She liked to pretend that he was in love with her, and in her fantasy she would turn and sing to him when they would play the love songs. He would mouth the words back to her; they had a special bond.

While she moved through the gym listening to her music, she was at first unaware of the other girls who were watching her. When the song finished, she looked up and saw the three of them, and she knew they were laughing at her. She must have been singing out loud again. She felt her face flush in embarrassment and moved more quickly to reach the door. She didn't have any close friends at school and always felt like the popular girls were watching her and thinking she was weird. One of the girls stepped in front of her, and she thought she was going to cry.

She was 10 years old, and she just never felt like she belonged anywhere. Her father was in the service, and her family moved all the time. As soon as she felt like she was beginning to make friends in one place, her family would move again. At home, she and her mother were alone most of the time. Her father worked long hours on the base and sometimes was away on business for a week at a time. When he would come home, her parents would spend most of their time fighting; sometimes her father would hit her mother and threaten to hit her if she tried to help. She was afraid of her father and would spend time in her room when he was home. In her room she felt safe, and she could imagine a world in which she was the popular girl everyone wanted to have as their friend. She had a vivid fantasy life that included her music and special characters on her television shows. She would conjure up images of herself as the heroine and would hurry home to daydream. She would listen to her music or watch one of her shows and get lost in a world of fantasy.

She was always worried about her mother. She wondered what would happen to her if her mother were to get sick and die. There would be no one to take care of her. Her mother always seemed to be in another world and didn't pay much attention to her. She wished that she had a brother or sister to play with and to sleep with at night when she was most afraid. Once, she had come home and had found her mother on the floor in the kitchen; she had not known what had happened, but her mother would not wake up. She had run next door to get a neighbor, and they had called an ambulance. She had to stay with her neighbor overnight until her mother came home. No one had ever told her what happened.

The girls at this school seemed worse than at other schools, where the kids would just ignore her. These girls seemed to want to pick on her, and she didn't have any idea what to do about it. When the girl stepped in front of her in the gym, she burst into tears. She felt afraid, alone, and trapped. She felt different and she believed that she would never belong anywhere because she was always new and didn't fit in with the crowd. One of the girls who blocked her way looked worried when she started to cry and told her friends to stop being bullies. The three girls let her pass, and she ran out of the gym into the school yard. She ran home, and no one was there, so she went into her room and turned on the music, getting lost in her daydreams and fantasies about being loved and popular.

This 10-year-old child was raised in a home environment of neglect. Her father was often unavailable, and when he was at home, he was sometimes abusive to her mother. She often felt afraid of her father, and when he was home, she would stay in her room as much as she could. Her mother was often drunk or sleeping due to her alcohol use. The child was moved often and had few friends because her family never stayed in one place for very long. She was an only child and did not have a close extended family with whom she could build healthy, loving bonds.

This child found that she was often in the position of caring for herself. At an early age, she had learned to dress herself and get ready for school. She was able to find what she needed to eat in the pantry when her mother slept late. Her emotional needs were addressed by the adults in her life.

As the years went by, this child had developed a coping mechanism of using fantasy to help ease her fear, sadness, and loneliness. When she was very young, she had played with her dolls, and as she got older, she lost herself in her music and fantasy. She liked to read and imagine herself as one of the characters in a happier place with a big family. Because depression can be a silent illness and she had not stayed in one place long enough for a teacher or other adult to notice that she was withdrawn, no one had intervened or reached out to her.

Looking back on her life she can remember always having felt very sad, except for when she was in her dream world. There were times when she learned from her parents that they were going to move once again when she would wish that she could just die instead of having to pack. She could clearly recall the incident when she was 10 years old and the girls in the new gym had tried to bully her. This was the first time that she had cut herself. These first cuts had not been deep, and she had covered the marks with long sleeves until they had healed. She used her fingernails or a sharp object, such as part of her pen, to make the cuts. As an adolescent, she continued to cut herself in places that no one would notice. Most of the time, she did not necessarily want to die, but she did want to inflict pain on herself. There were times, however, when she became so depressed that she did want to take her own life. She had a plan to leave a long note to her parents, telling them how much she hated her life and how much happier she would be if she could just go to sleep and not wake up. She knew her mother had medications she could take, and once she had taken a bunch of pills, but they had only made her feel sick to her stomach.

She moved into young adulthood with periods of dark depression that came and went. She stopped the cutting because she was ashamed of the scars, but she began to drink heavily. She was very attractive, and she had boyfriends, but they did not last. There were people in her workplace who she could have developed relationships with, but she did not initiate this companionship. She continued to feel isolated and alone; it was as if her childhood followed her everywhere, and she could not change things. She continued to use her fantasy world as a place of safety and hope. She would put her thoughts into writing, and she had a number of journals going at any one time.

When she was 24 and living alone, she drank several glasses of wine and decided to drive to the beach. She knew she should not drive under the influence, but she didn't care. As she drove, she found herself going faster and faster and again having that feeling that she did not want to live anymore. She impulsively pushed her pedal to the floor, and as she rounded a tight corner, the car flew off the road and crashed into a tree.

She woke up in the hospital with a broken collarbone and serious bruising. She was angry that she was alive. She couldn't stop crying. The hospital staff soon realized that she didn't have visitors and that she seemed to be depressed, so they had the hospital social worker visit her. It was clear to the social worker that she was suffering from clinical depression, in addition to her medical trauma.

This was the beginning of her journey to recovery. The hospital social work spent time with her in the hospital and helped her to put a name to the depression that she had been feeling all her life. She agreed to seek counseling when she was discharged. Her first several sessions were very uncomfortable for her because she had never been the focus of anyone's attention before and she hardly knew what to say to the therapist. After all, her parents had never hit her or been sexually abusive to her. She felt as though she must be making up her problems. Her counselor slowly helped her to see that she had been neglected and isolated all her life. The therapist helped her to begin to understand that neglect can be even more destructive than physical or sexual abuse because it is insidious. She was able to learn about her resiliencies with the counselor's help. She had survived; a plant with almost no water had grown in rocky soil. The counselor acted as the first mirror that she had ever had, and, as her therapist reflected herself back to her, she could begin to see herself in a positive light for the first time. She was referred for a trial of medication, and this, combined with her counseling, lifted her depression for the first time that she could remember. She began to use her fantasy world in a much more functional way by writing stories that she could publish, taking an early coping skill and building it into a second career. With the support of her therapist she joined a women's group and began to initiate social contacts with her colleagues. As she became educated regarding alcoholism and depression, she stopped her drinking completely and attended twelve-step meetings. Her resiliency grew as she utilized both old and new coping skills. She learned that if she felt suicidal or the urge to drink, these feelings were a new version of the earlier cutting she had done that was intended to cause herself pain.

Her vulnerabilities included parental neglect, possible biological predisposition to depression, genetic predisposition to alcoholism and later-life alcohol consumption, isolation, poor self-esteem, lack of familial and social supports, and her own depression, which was manifested in self-abusive behaviors and suicidality.

Her resiliencies included an active, positive fantasy life with music, writing, and daydreaming about a better life. She was also willing to seek counseling when it was offered, to build and utilize coping skills, and to stop alcohol consumption. Although she faced many vulnerabilities to suicidal predisposition, she also had several resilient qualities and an internal survival instinct that could be built upon and fortified.

■ Vulnerabilities to Adult Suicide

The development of suicidal thoughts and feelings can begin in the earliest stages of biological and personality formation, or they may emerge in one moment of great individual hopelessness. As discussed in chapter 2, the people who can be most vulnerable to suicidal ideation may have family histories laced with depression, suicidal gestures, or completed suicide(s). These individuals also may have grown up in early home environments in which they were abused or neglected. When interpersonal trust is violated at an early age, the victim can have great difficulty choosing later relationships that are well balanced and healthy. Unfortunately, a pattern can be established in which, according to Liz Grauerholz, early "victims may find themselves caught within social networks that are exploitive and that cause further reduction in the ability to trust others."[1] These individuals may choose partners and significant others who are similar to the early caregivers who were unkind, ambivalent, or abusive to them, and are, therefore, familiar. As a cycle of negative life experiences continues from childhood into adulthood, hope for change in the future diminishes. These people may isolate themselves and use avoidance patterns in their interactions, creating further vulnerabilities to loneliness, depression, and suicidal thought. Stevan Hobfoll describes loss spirals in resources such as social support; these spirals of loss can, in turn, damage the survivor's abilities to recover from traumatic events.[2] The early vulnerability factors that lead to adult depression and suicidality are powerful events to be overcome.

As the young child develops within his family and culture, his core being is formed. Vulnerabilities to a healthy, happy lifestyle are cultivated when the family of origin has biological or environmental hazards, such as medical illness or mental illness, or neglect or abuse toward the child.

The type of individual medical history that can compromise a child's well-being might include her own medical illness such as asthma, Lyme disease, leukemia, Crohn's disease, cerebral palsy, cancer, irritable bowel syndrome, congenital heart disease, or any other chronic or acute medical condition that affects the child's daily functioning. These medical conditions may limit or interfere with the child's interactions with others, including family, friends, and schoolmates. School may be missed, and this can result in academic struggles, which, in turn, can affect self-esteem. If the child's family system does not know how to assist the medically challenged child, vulnerabilities can manifest and grow. Medical vulnerability can be significant in the breeding of depression. As the child experiences feelings of powerlessness and difference from others due to her medical challenges, she may internalize feelings of sadness and hopelessness that can lead to depression and suicidal thought. Children with medical illness may carry a great deal of guilt over requiring so much attention from the family. These children can come to believe that they are an emotional and financial drain on the family. While they are medically ill, they also may experience emotional difficulties that can linger long after the illness has passed. These children can feel shame that their bodies are different than others in their peer group; for example, a child with Crohn's disease or irritable bowel syndrome may often be in need of using the bathroom at inopportune times. The need to stop activities for a bathroom break can feel embarrassing to these children, who want to appear to be like everyone else. A child with a medical illness will naturally be more tired than other children as her body uses more of its resources to compensate for the disease. She may wish to play as her peers do and can feel left on the sidelines when her body does not cooperate. The psychological aspects of medical issues can have great adverse impact on a growing youngster and may create serious vulnerability for depression.

A family member's medical illness also may create vulnerabilities for depression in a child. When someone else in the family system becomes chronically or acutely ill, all attention may be focused on that person, and not on the growing child. For example, if the mother in the family has cancer, family life will be focused around getting the mother to office visits and caring for this parent. The children in the family may experience deep and possibly realistic fears that their mother could die. These children may become isolated and unnoticed amid the medical crisis of the other family member. When a parent is ill, the children can experience great fears that they may be left alone. Some of the fears can become a reality when a parent is hospitalized and the child wonders whether the parent will ever come home again. Compounding these fears, when one parent is ill, the other parent often focuses all attention on the sick partner and has few emotional resources left to help the children understand and cope. The children may be left to guess and wonder about their sick parent and not have a clear or realistic understanding of the process of recovery. If the parent dies from the illness, another trauma befalls them as they deal with this grief.

When a sibling has a medical illness a similar scenario may take place. A sibling's medical illness can be complicated and create vulnerability for depression in its own way for the healthy child. The child who is well may feel survivor guilt that he has escaped the awful sickness that has consumed his brother or sister. At the same time, he may also fear that he could come down with the same illness that is harming his sibling. The healthy child may harbor some jealously that his sibling is getting all the attention, and he may feel guilty for having these feelings. Familial medical illness can create vulnerability in children for depression in early life or in later life. The child may manage to get through the period in which the family member is ill without showing signs of impact. Unless attention is provided to the needs of the child who remains well, however, symptoms could emerge later in time for this person. It can be terribly traumatic for a young person to watch a loved one with a catastrophic illness. When any family member is sick, generally much of the energy in the family is directed to the person who is ill. Unless a family or other elder is wise enough to notice and address the needs of the healthy family members, vulnerabilities are apt to arise for these individuals at some point in time, especially the children.

Mental illness in a child's family may also lead to early tendencies for depression. At times, the symptoms for depression that are reactive to familial mental illness may not manifest until later life, but the seeds may be sown early. Mental illnesses such as schizophrenia, bipolar disorder, Asperger's syndrome, obsessive-compulsive disorder, panic disorder, or a family member's depression can significantly affect a child's emotional state. The child may grow up an environment in which she does not have consistency and does not know what to expect from the behavior of her parent or sibling. In some cases, such as with schizophrenia, the behavior of the mentally ill family member may be bizarre or even violent. Some schizophrenic individuals hear voices that tell them to kill themselves or others. Imagine being a child in a family in which one of the parents or a sibling continually talks to himself and speaks of violent images or yells at the child for no apparent reason at all. Furthermore, imagine if the child in that home is routinely threatened by the schizophrenic person or told that the devil is coming to kill the whole family. The child will most likely feel terrified and confused. These children love their family member, yet they fear the mentally ill person, as well. Children with family members who have mental illness are affected emotionally. If they have a parent or sibling who is depressed, this can be as frightening in its own way as having a psychotic or schizophrenic family member. The child in the home with the depressed loved one may have heard threats of suicide and be fearful that her parent or sibling will commit suicide. The child may be witness to a parent staying in bed all the time or to a caregiver who self-medicates with alcohol or drugs. Mental illness in a family member can create vulnerability and depression in the child, especially if the child's needs and fears are unrecognized during the event of the illness. Families with mental illness constitute a double-edged sword of vulnerability for the child; there is both the emotional impact created by the illness and the genetic predisposition that is inherent in any family member of the mentally ill.

Other vulnerabilities include familial physical abuse, sexual abuse, substance abuse, neglect, poverty, and racism. Clearly, each of these circumstances can have a profound impact on a developing child and create a legacy for issues such as poor self-esteem, anger, sadness, isolation, and fear. In turn, each of these issues may be a causal factor that leads to suicidal thought or intent.

Childhood vulnerabilities may lead the developing youngster to feelings of despondency and learned helplessness. The individual may develop into an adult who can see little hope. Conversely, this adult may harbor deep feelings of rage and anger, which disrupt her ability to function in a healthy way in the world. As the negative cycle grows, the individual's responses to the world become based on the early environment that began in her family of origin.

Following are specific vulnerabilities to adult suicidality:

- History of family physical illness
- History of family mental illness
- Child physical abuse
- Child sexual abuse
- Child neglect
- No "important other"
- Traumatic event
- Loss
- Disrupted relationships (divorce, multiple partners)

- Hopelessness and rage that affects functioning
- Childhood mental illness or physical illness
- Early family conflict
- Low socioeconomic status
- Substance abuse (self or family member)
- Exposure to racism
- Absence of parental supervision
- Use of age-inappropriate media

The developing self is sensitive to the environment, and negative factors can be easily internalized. For example, the child who is raised in a family that provides limited supervision and interaction may lead to this child's feeling unlovable. This isolated child may entertain himself with media and find himself choosing programming that is laced with violence, sexuality, or a skewed view of the world. As the child comes to have a belief that he is not worthy of others' attention, he also may be filling up his knowledge of the world with the media's images of violence, sexuality, and a distorted idea of intimate relationships. If the child becomes focused on violent media images, he may internalize violence and believe that aggression is a proper behavioral response in his interactions with others. Isolation, feelings of worthlessness, anger due to caregiver ambivalence, and aggression reactive to media images can combine to create a powerful environment that can breed violence against self or others.

Conversely, if the isolated child is one who instead focuses on fantasy, her young mind may become laced with romantic images and a world that does not truly exist. Both the child who entertains himself with aggressive images and the child who watches fantasy have been left by their otherwise occupied caregivers to design their own set of beliefs about the world around them. None of these beliefs are based in full reality. These children may become vulnerable either to acts of violence against others or self, or they can be vulnerable to others who may prey on them. These vulnerabilities may lead to depression and suicidal thought or action.

A child who is raised in poverty is also vulnerable to depression and subsequent suicidal predisposition. This child may be raised in a home in which there is not enough to eat or the nutrition is not sufficient to promote proper body and brain function. The child may feel shame that his clothing is old and does not fit correctly; he may be cold and not have the needed outerwear to keep warm. There may be little or no electricity in the home to heat the building or to cook warm meals. Many of the privileges that most people take for granted can be elusive to those who live in poverty. Compounding the lack of resources, the impoverished child may experience feelings of embarrassment, fear, and prejudice from others. The feelings of shame and need from early years of poverty can follow a child throughout his life, creating low self-worth and subsequent depression.

In a home in which there are unstable or multiple relationships between the adults, a sensation of disconnectedness or attachment disruption can exist for the children who live there. As discussed in chapter 1, violent relationships, including physical, sexual, and verbal abuse, can have both an immediate and long-standing impact on a child's emotional well-being. Children can be affected by a parent who has multiple partners with whom they become attached and then lose. If this kind of significant loss occurs many times in a young person's life, she may come to believe that her parent's partners are leaving because of her. She may feel or believe that she is not lovable enough for the other adult to stay, and her self-esteem can be affected greatly. When a child is raised in a single-parent home and the caregiver has multiple partners but does not recognize the impact that this can have on the child, vulnerabilities are created. These young people can become vulnerable to sadness and depression, triggered by repetitive loss.

Vulnerability for depression can be created by a traumatic event in the life of a child or young person who has not yet developed the appropriate resources to cope with the event. Examples of traumatic events include tragic accidents in which there is death or serious injury, seeing a loved one being harmed or die, witnessing extreme violence, witnessing a friend drown, being abandoned, or held without consent. Many other kinds of trauma can significantly affect a child's emotional well-being that may not initially appear to be as damaging as some others. However, any event or series of events that causes a negative ripple effect on a child ultimately can foster vulnerability for depression. For example, if an attached, sensitive child loses a pet and then experiences the loss of a beloved grandparent, the combined events could lead to despair.

Childhood vulnerabilities to depression are numerous and can have a lasting effect on both the child and her journey to adulthood. Although there are many ways in which an individual can become vulnerable, there are equally as many resources with which resiliencies to protect against vulnerabilities and resulting depression can be built and broadened.

■ Challenging Destiny: Human Resiliency

The human spirit is the one of the most resilient and amazing phenomena of our fragile existence. Time and again, under the most horrific circumstances, evidence shows that individuals can survive and even thrive. In the lifetime of every person some incident or trial will test the core strength of that person's being. The level of stress that the specific trial may bring is relative. For example, a divorce is always stressful and involves upheaval, even in the best of circumstances. How the parties involved manage the stress can depend on the resiliency of the individual. Early childhood neglect and abuse create a foundation for the individual upon which all other stressors fall. The more resilient the person, the greater her adaptive functioning will be in the world when other negative life stressors befall her. Divorce, major illness, physical illness, tragic accidents, loss of a loved one, job loss, war, and a myriad of other tragedies can befall the adult. When these issues are compounded by the early vulnerabilities of abuse, neglect, or tragedy, the effects can be potentially catastrophic if the individual is not resilient.

George Bonanno described resiliency as a dynamic process of healthy adaptation in the face of severe adversity.[3] The resiliency of the human spirit has been seen in even the most soul-destroying circumstances. The world has been witness to individuals who have survived the Holocaust, the bombings of Hiroshima and Nagasaki, world wars, and extreme personal suffering and poverty. These individuals not only have survived unbelievable trauma, but many also have gone on to lead productive lives that have had a positive impact on others and on society. How is it possible for some to have the emotional and spiritual capacity to recover sufficiently from tragedy to function effectively in life? Why do others fall into despair and lose all hope?

Jon Shaw reports that during childhood, even when the environment is not optimal for the development of a healthy self, some internal resiliencies may be the result of unknown genetic determinants. Genetic resiliency factors are internal biological and personality characteristics with which the infant is born that can help some individuals move forward and prosper even when they have faced what can appear to be insurmountable odds.[4]

These inherent genetic traits that can fortify a sense of hope even in extraordinarily bleak conditions are mysterious and as yet undefined by research. Remarkably, some infants who are born into miserable circumstances have an intrinsically better ability to thrive than others born into the same set of circumstances. Genetic resiliency is an area in which information is sparse. Research into the neuropsychological pathways of the infant is needed. Further information could provide a wealth of understanding in explaining how some infants intrinsically are born better fortified to withstand trauma than are other newborns.

Although the genetic origins of resiliency may be mysterious, the environmental factors that contribute to surviving and thriving are much clearer. These elements are generally referred to as protective factors and can result in child and adult adaptive behaviors under adverse circumstances. Many environmental protective factors can help an individual to be resilient. Diane Papalia, Sally Wendos Olds, and Ruth Feldman describe one of the most important elements in developing resiliency as having a supportive environment.[5] As previously discussed, many of the early vulnerability factors for suicide are the result of children living in homes in which the caregivers fail to provide a safe or consistent environment. If a child is raised by caregivers who are attuned and attentive, internal resiliency will be established as mental health issues or suicidal tendencies are managed in a loving and caring manner. However, the child or infant who is raised by unaware or abusive caregivers begins life at an extraordinary disadvantage. A powerful protective factor for this disadvantaged infant or child would be to have at least one other person in his environment with whom he can feel safe, esteemed, or hopeful. This "important other" could be a distant relative, a teacher, a grandparent, or a neighbor. Even when contact with a caring adult may be limited and appear to be superficial, the meaning that the child can make from a positive interaction with one adult can have a profoundly reparative effect on an abused or neglected child. The relationship that a child can have with an important other can foster some of the positive experiences that the child may be lacking in the home environment. Words of praise from a teacher, a kind gesture from an extended family member, an invitation to a neighbor's dinner table, and words of support can increase a child's positive sense of self. According to Katey Baruth and Jane Carroll, the important others in a child's life become even more crucial when the child is not experiencing positive interactions at home. Resilient individuals are likely to have a family member, friend, or encouraging community member who provides a trusted and supportive environment or relationship.[6]

Additionally, a child's perception of a supportive other can also provide positive effects. For example, a teacher may have kind words for all members of a class, but the vulnerable child may perceive that the words from the teacher are meant for him alone. Results from a study by Jeremiah Schumm, Melissa Phillips, and Stevan Hobfoll on interpersonal trauma and resiliency suggest that social support may buffer the cumulative effect of child and adult interpersonal trauma and that perceived social support serves a buffering role for survivors of child abuse and adult rape.[7] Interactions with a positive adult role model can clearly help to provide a sense of hope for youngsters, even if the contact with the important other is limited. A child may have access to a kind and supportive grandparent only once or twice a year; however, this support may be meaningful enough to help the child feel a sense of being loved and esteemed by someone in the world. These positive feelings can improve self-esteem and self-efficacy, and promote overall well-being in the child. The impact of the positive important other in the life of an abused or neglected child cannot be minimized. In fact, little kindnesses that others can provide in the early years foster hope and resilience and improve the individual's ability to combat despair and suicidal tendencies throughout the life span.

According to Diane Papalia, along with having an important other to help foster resiliency, the impact of having compensating experiences can be instrumental in fortifying strength and survival in the child and in later years in the adult.[8] Compensating experiences are events in which the child or adult is able to achieve attainable goals. These goals may be clearly set markers or may be naturally developing mastery over life's transitional events. For example, the very young child will feel pleasure when she is able to grasp and hold an object that previously has been out of her ability to hold. The older child will feel a sense of accomplishment as she becomes successful in mastering her environment and play. For a developing child, building a tower of blocks or learning to tie her shoes can be a matter of great self-pride. Additionally, when a child is able to complete a task successfully, this is a marker to her that she is competent. This feeling of mastery is based on what is visible and concrete; even if the child does not receive positive feedback from the caregiver, she bears witness to her own success. These compensating experiences can begin in early childhood and continue as the child successfully completes the developmental stages of growth. As the compensating experiences grow, so does the child's knowledge that she is bright, competent, and successful. The child's self-esteem improves from her own positive outcomes, and resiliency to outside forces develops and strengthens.

Even for adults, compensating experiences can be especially helpful in building and maintaining resiliency. If an adult has repeated failures in one area of his life but also has reparative, successful experiences in another area, he will be more likely to retain a positive sense of self. This positive sense of well-being, in turn, fosters resiliency and a better ability to manage the effects of failure.

Positive experiences with friendship can also help both children and adults to feel an improved sense of self. Friendships help the child to build an internal understanding that she can have fulfilling relationships. These early peer relationships can be crucial factors in compensating for limited positive responses from the child's caretaker. A child who does not receive attention or positive response at home but who develops early friendships may be able to internalize important experiences of love from her companions. Although her home life may be barren of much-needed affection, seeds of warmth can be garnered from the environment through friendships that may create hope and fill the empty soul. Both in childhood and in later adulthood, friends can take on the role of important others and may be a great source of support. As the child or adult feels esteem through the eyes of a friend, this positive regard helps the vulnerable individual to flourish. Friendships foster resiliency and decrease depression and isolation. Friendships are a protective factor against depression and subsequent completed suicide.

Diane Papalia and others attribute having an adaptable personality as another protective factor.[9] The infant or child with an adaptable temperament is more likely to be resilient under adverse circumstances. An infant is born with any number of characteristics that are unique to him, which make up his unique and individual temperament. These traits, which are present at birth, are hard-wired in the infant's brain and help to organize the child's approach to the world. Because of this wiring, some infants may have the innate ability to withstand a neglectful environment with greater positive outcomes than other infants experiencing the same kind of negative early experience. Science and research clearly inform us of how the child's genetics, culture, and environment play a part in how the child responds to its world. The formation of innate temperament traits, however, may be some of the more mysterious components to the development of the infant. As with genetics, further research is needed to address the differences in temperament that accompany the infant into the world.

Some infants are born with irritable, finicky, nervous, and distressed characteristics that make up their temperament. The infant with these personality characteristics is more vulnerable to continued difficulties in later life. Unfortunately, because their personalities require more sustained attention from their caretakers, these infants and children are more susceptible to increased abuse or neglect. As the infant with a distressed temperament whines and cries out its unknown frustrations, the caregiver can become exhausted and overwhelmed and may be unable to be attentive in a positive manner. This finicky infant may then have further difficulty adapting to the inconsistencies of the challenged caregiver, which can, in turn, result in an increase in the child's needs. A negative cycle can be created between child and parent, and abuse or neglect may heighten in response to the demands of the child. The little person who is born with distressed characteristics enters the world at a disadvantage. Ultimately, this infant can be more vulnerable to disrupted early relationships that may affect later adult functioning and lead to subsequent depression and suicidal predisposition.

   Conversely, the infant born with an adaptable temperament is more equipped to survive and grow even in a less-than-optimal environment. This small person seems to have the innate capacity to minimize the internal impact of negative experiences and, in a manner of speaking, roll with the punches. This infant is born into the world with the ability to survive chaos and unpredictability more easily than the previously described nervous infant. The adaptable infant and child greet the world with less intensity and distractibility, less irritability, greater mood stability, and a core of persistence. This infant is less likely to draw the wrath of the caregiver and, thus, may minimize the effects of abuse. With an adaptable personality, an infant draws others to him like moths to a flame. He coos and gurgles and entertains adults with his easy style. When there are parenting failures, this infant appears to be less apt to suffer the consequences.

   As stated, birth temperament is somewhat mysterious. The infant's temperament may not be tied at all to the parenting or birth environment of the child. At times, it appears to be a random phenomenon whether a child is born with a distressed, finicky personality or with an easy, affable personality. The consequences of birth temperament, however, can be life altering.

   A child who is born with an adaptable nature fosters and builds resilience throughout the life span. The person who is adaptable and has the ability to experience trauma without becoming overwhelmed by it will have improved functioning in all his daily routines and life events. This ability to be adaptable can help an individual move through the kind of depression and hopelessness that can lead to suicidal tendencies. Although the adaptable person may still be faced with trauma, stress, and feelings of despair, he will be more resilient in the management of life's inevitable turmoil.

   Papalia and others note as a final protective factor: the infant who is born into an environment with fewer stressors is more resilient than the infant who is born into a home of chaos and upheaval.[10] Furthermore, individuals throughout the life span appear to be less vulnerable to depression and subsequent suicide when life stressors are kept to a minimum. Michelle Dumont and Marc Provost's research has shown that "resilient persons" are likely to have experienced fewer life stressors and risk factors when compared with less resilient individuals.[11] Common sense dictates that a person who goes through life with few challenges may have an easier time of surviving and thriving than another person who may have many life obstacles to surmount. A child who has enough to eat, warm clothing, parental affection and consistency, and the opportunity for an education will not have the same hurdles to overcome that the underprivileged child faces. The growing individual with less internal and environmental stress will develop a sturdy sense of self, which is a strong protective factor against suicidal predisposition.

Protective factors may be cultural in nature. Cultural identification can increase a sense of belonging, social support, and adaptive functioning. Phillip Bowman said, "[c]ultural strengths facilitate adaptive coping and, in turn, well-being and health; and multilevel cultural strengths promote role resiliency by reducing risky cognitive analyses such as role discouragement, self-blame and hopelessness." Bowman goes on to state that "protective cultural strengths help to explain why some at risk youth maintain a sense of hope, vitality and persistence and excel against discouraging odds. Cultural strengths may reduce feelings of being overwhelmed, cut off or dispirited."[12] Religious and spiritual affiliations also can provide the individual with a sense of meaning and belonging. For a vulnerable youngster, the connection to a community church not only can provide an escape from home, but also may instill meaning and hope in an existence that otherwise could feel emotionally barren.

As noted, numerous protective factors can buffer the individual's vulnerabilities to suicidal tendencies. Environmental, adaptive, social, religious, and cultural factors can help the child who is living in an environment that is abusive or neglectful to develop and build resiliencies that can help her to function in the world. Many children do survive and master vulnerabilities when one or more protective factors are in place. The child may have an important other who helps to build her sense of self, she may have a strong sense of culture or ethnicity that gives her purpose, or she may have an adaptable personality that helps her to minimize the negative impact of her environment. Each protective factor acts as a shield against hopelessness and despair, which can lead to suicidal thought. Protective factors build resiliency for the current obstacles the child may face in life and for the events to come.

Interestingly, the strength and resiliency of an individual are often seen most clearly in the wake of a personal tragedy or loss. Once an individual experiences a tragic event and is able to cope with the aftermath of the event and the accompanying feelings, he may then experience a sense of mastery and a knowledge that he can survive. This can be a powerful realization and bring with it a feeling of hope that he will be able to cope with any further life travails. Self-efficacy and optimism are both important elements in resilience. According to Karen Reivich and Andrew Shatte, hope is a crucial element in combating despair, and when an individual is able to survive and master a traumatic event, his ability to hope can be fortified.[13] The fortification of an individual's hope further strengthens his resilience for the challenges that life will certainly present.

▪ Building and Fortifying Resiliencies

External and internal mechanisms can be utilized to build resiliency in vulnerable individuals. If the seeds for resiliency can be planted early in the life of the individual, then it is less likely that this person will develop suicidal tendencies in later life.

Externally Built Resiliency

External mechanisms for building hope, strength, and adaptability in children can come from the important others or the community. The earlier the intervention occurs, the greater the positive impact will be on the child. Often, the adult who has great influence on a child and who is an important other does not have a clear understanding that he or she is fulfilling such a crucial role. Therefore, to increase the resiliency that develops within the child from the intervention of an external source, an awareness of the impact of these forces must be increased. For example, the teacher who has a kind word for a quiet child may not realize just how crucial these words can be; the loving grandparent might not understand that comforting words can make all the difference in the world of a small child. Some children have the first consistent and nurturing experience in their lives in church, afterschool programs, sports, or other school-sponsored activities. These vulnerable children often attempt to escape their dysfunctional home circumstances by spending as much time as possible at school. The wise educator understands that these children need more from them than formal education; they need encouragement and words of support. What may seem to be small inconsequential kindnesses in some circumstances can have a monumental impact on a developing self that is hungry for attention and praise. The school is a place that a child can experience positive reparative interactions with adults and begin to hear alternative perspectives than what she is exposed to at home.

Church, a community recreation program, or another sponsored program may also be places that can have a significant positive impact on the world of a vulnerable child. A camp counselor who reaches out and spends a few extra moments with a quiet child may begin to show this child that he is lovable and worthy of attention. A spiritual leader or church member who redirects a child who is acting out toward a new set of behaviors may unknowingly be one of the only adults to have taken this initiative with the youngster.

Providing positive attention to children may seem to make simple common sense; unfortunately, this is not always the way that youngsters are treated in the world. Some educators and community leaders may be overwhelmed by the level of need they see in these children and may not have the skills or resources to manage the emotional issues that these special young people bring to the classroom and community. At times, youth can be further victimized in the community as their behaviors are misunderstood as inattention or rebellion.

Training programs in the schools and community are often available to help providers identify and assist children who are vulnerable and at risk for depression and hopelessness. These training programs are valuable reminders for providers of how a simple action by an external resource can make a significant difference in a child's life and subsequent development. Ongoing, free caregiver classes may be provided in communities to address the basics of raising a healthy and happy child. Local workshops for the general public that review the basics of listening and providing feedback to children are useful for anyone who provides care to children. These workshops may be offered in the church, library, or school; listings for the topic, time, and date of these workshops may be found in the local newspaper or online. Some of the information that is provided at these workshops and trainings may seem simple; however, the act of attending and being reminded that the use of basic strategies to assist children grow into healthy adults can be crucial. The community workshops that teach such topics as promoting self-esteem in children or listening skills also provide an opportunity for adults to network and build their own support systems. These networks can be a wonderful resource for other opportunities that may be available in the community. Supportive relationships may be formed by those in attendance, and word-of-mouth referrals to other training programs propel the continuum of good care for our children.

When the primary caregivers are not available to provide a consistent and loving home environment for their children, it becomes the responsibility of every other adult in that child's life to step forward. Even if it is only for a moment, any small positive intervention can have a lasting impact on the child. When positive external resources are present for the child either in the home, school, church, or community, resiliency strategies are imparted to help the child manage distress. As these external resources expand to multiple sources that provide positive feedback to the child, the early risk factors that ultimately can lead to suicidal tendencies may be mitigated.

Internally Built Resiliency

Internal mechanisms for developing resiliencies come from within, although seeds may be planted from external sources. These internal mechanisms are either personality based or develop over time as the child grows into an adult. Some internal elements of resilience include developing strong coping skills, having a sense of humor, setting and achieving goals, changing automatic negative thoughts, developing purpose and meaning in life, and having hope. The foundation for the development of such positive internal resources may be imparted by an important other or learned by the adaptable child.

Internal coping skills include many strategies that can be crucial for the individual's emotional and physical survival in an abusive world. For the young child, coping with an unpredictable life may mean developing skills that provide physical safety. At a very early age, children can gain the understanding that they need to remain quiet or stay in their room when the caregivers are intoxicated or raging. This withdrawal to safety is considered to be a coping skill and may come from an internal sense of survival. The child who learns to put herself out of harm's way and to stay safe is positively reinforced by avoiding the pain of a beating or verbal abuse. The positive reinforcement leads to a continuation of the behavior of withdrawal and, thus, to further safety. While withdrawal may not be a functional adult coping mechanism, in an abusive child's life, it is a very good strategy. As the child grows, her coping skills may develop to include staying later at school or spending as much time at a friend's home as possible.

Another learned and developed coping skill is presenting a compliant self to the world. While many children in abusive or neglectful homes feel anger and sadness, they learn to hide these feelings and show the world a false happy face. In this way, they may keep the parent satisfied and further keep themselves from the potential wrath of their caregiver. Children in abusive and neglectful homes tend to be hypervigilant and generally are very aware of the mood of their caretaker. If they detect that their parent is in an abusive mood, they will adapt their personality to match a mood that will please and soothe the caretaker. Once again, while in adulthood compliance is not necessarily a functional trait, in an unpredictable home the child uses this strategy to remain safe.

Children in unsafe environments may also adapt themselves to becoming the home caretaker. They may need to care for and protect younger siblings and keep them quiet when they perceive the adult is drunk or apt to be abusive. They may need to take on the role of the adult by getting themselves and their brothers and sisters up for school, making sure there is something to eat, and keeping the home clean. This role of parentified child is another functional coping skill for children in abusive environments. As they master the skills needed to keep daily routines and to stay fed, clean, and safe, they build internal resiliency. They master an unsafe environment.

Some children cope and, oddly enough, build internal resiliency by living in a fantasy world. These children may bury themselves in books, music, television, and other electronic devices such as digital movies and music players. Their fantasy lives provide them with distance from their painful real worlds and also can provide them with hope. As these children view the media version of how other families live their lives, they may come to believe that life can be different. Their immersion in fantasy may keep them partially protected from the harsh reality that may be their world.

Although these coping skills may not be thought of as positive resources, for the child these skills are functional and help to keep her safe in her unsafe world. Indeed, these strategies not only keep the child out of harm's way, but also provide an additional inner strength as she learns that there is hope, that she can master her environment even when it is dangerous, and that she can survive treacherous circumstances. The knowledge that she can manage her life a harrowing environment creates an internal resiliency and the knowledge that she can survive.

As these youngsters grow into adulthood, some of these early coping strategies will no longer be functional. The coping patterns for survival that were developed by these young minds and that helped to build internal resiliency in childhood will no longer be viewed as positive internal resources. In fact, some of the strategies that these young people used and mastered to keep safe will affect them in adulthood in negative ways. For example, living in a fantasy world or being compliant as an adult may not help an adult individual to flourish, and, in fact, could have a negative impact on an adult's life. These adults will need to learn new and more effective methods of managing adversity. Unfortunately, some early patterns of development are challenging to change, and it may require the help of a counselor to design new and healthier life patterns.

Another important internal resource for any child is both cognitive and emotional intelligence. A bright child will quickly learn patterns that can keep her from harm and may be less likely to repeat behaviors that will cause her to be threatened by the caregiver. When a child is bright, she will easily pick up the nuances from the adults in her world. The ability to grasp what the caregiver expects from her and the cognitive knowledge to respond appropriately helps the child to receive positive energy from her parent. Intelligence that results from a high intelligence quotient (IQ) leads to cognitive strengths; the child will have a stronger chance of understanding what she needs to do and have the ability to then respond in a fashion that reaps her rewards. These children will quickly learn to mimic the behaviors that get them the desired response.

Children with good emotional intelligence may fare better in their environment. These children understand with a high degree of complexity the emotional world around them and respond accordingly. The child who is emotionally bright will pick up on a parent's sadness or internal emotional state and match his own personality in response. This is not the same strategy the hypervigilant child uses when afraid and who then becomes compliant or withdrawn; rather, this is a child who comprehends the emotional state of his world and reacts accordingly. The result of being a child with a higher state of emotional intelligence is that the adults surrounding him may feel understood and, thus, drawn in a positive way to the child.

Having a higher cognitive or emotional intelligence can promote a child's sense of humor. Humor is generally found in children who are bright, and humor can be a protective factor as it keeps the individual's spirits up even in adverse circumstances. The child who is able to laugh and find amusement in her world will move through life more easily than one who is unable to use this cognitive strength. As the child matures, humor can lead the young person to understand paradox in adversity, and this understanding can be a protective factor against otherwise bleak circumstances. Humor is an internal resource that builds resiliency. Additionally, when a child has a sense of humor, she tends to be better liked by others in her environment, and this likability can provide a secondary advantage of safety.

Finally, hope is an internal resource that builds resiliency. The ability to hope that a positive outcome will be eventual is essential to ensure emotional well-being. If hope does not exist, despair and despondency can form and solidify a toxic inner world. The ability to hope that life will be different and to believe that painful circumstances can change can make any current conflict more manageable. Hope is the antidote to hopelessness. Hope may be an elusive concept to a child caught in a family cycle of violence and chaos, but for those children who are able to find and hold on to hope, the ability to withstand their family dysfunction and be resilient is magnified.

How does hope develop and grow in some and diminish in others? The presence of at least one of the protective factors that have been discussed may lead a child to find a seed of hope and cling to it. This seed of hope can be cultivated as the child moves into the outer world and sees that not all families or circumstances are bleak and that the potential exists for kindness and positive responses from others in the world. Hope can flourish as the child sees the world through the media; although the media may not project a real-life image of how all families act, it offers alternatives to the belief that all homes are abusive.

Positive expectations, or hope, closely relate to the concept of self-efficacy. Self-efficacy refers to the expectation that one's behavior will be effective.[14] When someone believes that he can have an impact on his environment, this hope leads to action; therefore, feelings of helplessness decrease. Children who can hope are more apt to successfully combat depression and subsequent suicidal tendencies. They are able to believe that their lives will improve; they trust that somehow the abuser will stop the abuse, that they will be loved, or that someone will rescue them. The internal ability to hope fosters the desire to survive. Hope is a powerful friend to building and maintaining resiliency and is a crucial antidote to despair.

The following chapter will detail specific methods of recovery and coping strategies for the suicidal person. For those individuals who have some internal and external resiliency factors already in place, the recovery process may be easier. Resiliency factors can be developed and learned at any stage of the life span, however, even when vulnerabilities are great. Chapter 4 spells out a specific common-sense plan to recovery from depression and suicidal intent.

4 ▪ ▪ ▪

Hope for Those with Suicidal Predisposition

▪ Case Example: The Dark Room

Julia was having a bad day. Her 45th birthday celebration had been the previous night, and she had enjoyed the evening with her husband and friends, but today she felt sluggish and unmotivated. She had been noticing for the past several weeks that she was beginning to have difficulty falling asleep at night and getting out of bed in the morning. Her husband had commented recently that she seemed preoccupied and distant. Julia was aware that she was beginning to slip back into the place that she had nicknamed the dark room, and she knew she needed to take some steps to keep from locking herself in that familiar place.

Julia had learned long ago that she was a person who could easily succumb to depression. She had had a tremendously painful childhood, and although she had survived it, without her attention there were scars that could easily open and become infected. Julia had learned not to spend too much time recalling her early years; when she thought about her childhood, she could get caught in a trap of cyclic negative memories that created nothing for her but emotional pain.

Julia had been born into a family that kept secrets. She had been taught not to talk to others outside the family and to keep her feelings to herself. Her mother was an alcoholic, and by the time Julia was five, she had become the caretaker in the family. She would look after her little brother, make sure that he was fed and changed, and even try to make her mother eat and go to bed. At age five Julia had been very bright and cute. She had known how to stay out of her mother's way when her moods would shift. Julia would take her brother with her to play games in another room, away from their mother's potential anger, which could harm them. She could remember being afraid that she might not be able to feed her brother because there was not enough food in the cabinet. Sometimes they ate only cereal, and many times there was nothing to drink but water. Julia could not recall her father. For many years Julia had thought that her family was like everyone else's family.

Her mother had many boyfriends. They were generally nice to Julia and her brother in the beginning; then it seemed that they would lose interest in them. At first, Julia had thought that one of the boyfriends might marry their mother and it would be like a Disney movie; they would be taken care of and loved. But after many men had passed in and out of the apartment, Julia figured out that these men just didn't care about her. Once, when her mother was passed out in the living room, one of the men had come into the room that Julia shared with her brother. The man told her to be quiet and not to tell when he touched her. He came into her room many times, and Julia knew that her mother would not stop him. This man had stayed with her mother longer than the others, and he had made sure that they had food and got to school on time. There were many loud fights between her mother and the man at night, and Julia knew that after a fight the man would come to her room. She had never liked to use his name and still thought of his as "the man." These were the years that Julia began to feel like she was in a dark room that she could not escape.

Julia's brother would come home much later than her after school on the bus, so every day Julia had time to herself to visit her neighbor, Miss Harper, who lived on the first floor. She would wait there and watch out the window for her brother's bus to arrive. Julia loved to go to Miss Harper's apartment. Miss Harper would always have a snack ready for her, and she would sit on her couch and listen to Miss Harper's stories. Julia would cozy up on the couch, and sometimes Miss Harper would put her arm around Julia or cover her with a warm blanket. Julia's memories of Miss Harper were the best ones she could remember. Julia wished she lived with Miss Harper all the time. She would sometimes watch from the window in her own upstairs apartment and would see when Miss Harper went out to shop or do errands. When Julia got older, she would help Miss Harper shovel the walkway and sometimes make snacks to eat. They would watch the same soap opera on television together every day, and Julia smiled when she thought that she still liked to watch that program sometimes.

It seemed to Julia, in looking back, that once she had realized that there were people and families in the world who could show affection and kindness like Miss Harper, she had had a harder time wanting to wake up. The dark room had become darker. She could remember consciously thinking at a young age that she wished she would just go to sleep and right to heaven.

Julia could clearly remember the first time she had decided that she wanted to die. She had been 14. The sexual abuse had stopped when she was 11; one day, the man just never came back. Her mother's drinking seemed to be the same; she would pass out on the couch, and it really was as if Julia was the mother. Julia thought she could make sure that here brother would be taken care of if she died by writing a letter to her uncle who lived in California. Julia wrote the letter and mailed it. Julia had not been quite sure how to die, but she thought that if she took all her mother's pills, she would go to sleep and not wake up. Julia thought her mother would never know if she didn't wake up, and there would be enough time for Julia to go to sleep forever. The day that Julia had mailed the letter to her uncle she took a full bottle of medication that was in her mother's cabinet. She remembered that she had felt very calm and settled with her decision.

Instead of falling asleep, Julia became very, very ill. She experienced extraordinary stomach cramping, and the pain was so bad that she went for help to Miss Harper, who called an ambulance. Julia's mother was not at home.

Julia remembered that this was the first of several suicide attempts that she made between the time she was age 14 and age 22. She had been hospitalized twice for her attempts. Once, Julia had cut her wrists so deeply that she still wore longer sleeves when she wanted to hide the scars. She had been assigned a counselor, but Julia had learned not to tell her family secrets, so the counselor had not really understood. Julia had liked going to counseling because she had felt safe there, but she had not shared her deep pain or the level of depression she was feeling. When Julia was 18, she had her first boyfriend, and she fell in love with him. This had been the most important relationship Julia had ever known. When he broke up with her, she was devastated and had known she had a final choice. She was either going to kill herself or try to do something to stop the negative thought patterns that seemed to be poisoning her mind.

For the first time, Julia had sought help from a counselor herself. The counselor was a warm woman who had wanted Julia to call her

Ginny. Ginny was very skilled in understanding and working with the kind of pain a young woman like Julia was carrying inside her. Julia slowly had opened up to Ginny about her past. Ginny assessed Julia and determined that Julia was most likely suffering from a depression that was both biological in nature and exaggerated by environmental factors. Although Julia had been diagnosed with depression when she was younger, she had not understood or cared what that meant. This time, Julia had wanted to see if she could stop the suicidal thoughts and feel better about herself and her life. Ginny referred Julia to a psychiatric nurse practitioner, who could provide Julia with the correct medication to decrease her depression. Julia began to sleep better at night. She found that her appetite improved and that she was able to stop some of the negative thoughts with the skills that Ginny taught her. When she had felt suicidal, or if the negative thoughts returned, Julia learned to use self-soothing techniques to fill up the empty space inside her. She and Ginny had an agreement that if Julia felt she was going to harm herself, she would call either Ginny or the Suicide Help Line. Over time, Ginny helped Julia to see that she was a good and lovable person. Julia experienced moments of great sadness and loss in her therapy regarding her childhood, but she also recalled Miss Harper and how comforted she had felt by this kind woman. Julia began to take the memories of the warmth from Miss Harper and use these memories when she needed to feel loved. She also began to build present-day supports in her life with others who were equally as loving and available.

Today, Julia knew when she was having a bad day. She recognized the signs of her depression, and she knew what she needed to do for herself. She called her new therapist, someone she needed to see only now and then. She set up an appointment and realized that she might need to go back on medication for a period of time. Julia had learned that once the symptoms of depression began, she needed to take action before she became suicidal. Julia was familiar with the emotional triggers that could lead to her depression, such as the darker winter months or stress. She did not want to return to the dark room. She knew she needed to call for help.

■ There Is Hope

Suicidal predisposition is not a fatal diagnosis for completed suicide. Many individuals with suicidal thoughts and behaviors are able to recover and to lead healthy, adaptive lives. Understanding and intervention can alter negative life experiences that may lead some individuals who are born and raised with suicidal vulnerabilities to recovery.

Depression is a treatable illness with an excellent recovery rate when help is obtained.

Each individual's experience and recovery can be different from another's experience and recovery. There is no specific map for recovery; each person is unique and has a unique set of experiences; therefore, each recovery plan should be adapted to the individual's needs and life history.

Some individuals reach out for help at the first suicidal thought. They may feel frightened by the images of their own death and have an instinct of self-preservation that propels them to reach out for assistance. Asking for help and telling someone about suicidal thoughts is an important step in the recovery process.

The people who develop support systems can use these resources when the feelings of self-harm become overwhelming. Once a professional is included in the support network, the suicidal individual will have clinical resources that can further decrease suicidal intent. The professional will assist the suicidal person in developing a safety plan and fortifying a support network to use when needed. Cognitive interventions and medication may be suggested by the professional to reduce suicidality. Clinical research indicates that the reduction of suicidal symptoms is dramatic in depressed individuals who receive both psychotherapy and medication.

Some individuals with depression may have experienced suicidal images for many years, never telling anyone. Eventually, these individuals' suicidal thoughts may escalate to suicidal gestures and planned intent for self-harm. Important others surrounding these suicidal people may not be aware of the distress these individuals are experiencing and may be deeply surprised when a suicide attempt is made. Although a person experiencing depression generally exhibits signs, these signs may be subtle and not easily recognized or understood to be taken seriously. Depression is sometimes referred to as a "silent killer" because it can be so lethal, and the symptoms of hopelessness and withdrawal may go unrecognized.

Once depression is identified and suicidal thoughts are uncovered, it is crucial that supports be put in place. The supports that can lead to recovery may vary, depending n the circumstances and wishes of the person. Recognizing suicidal tendencies, external resources, strategies, and coping skills that can be helpful to the suicidal individual will be described in detail in the next several pages.

■ Recognizing Suicidal Tendencies: When You Need Help

Depression can begin slowly and be experienced as low-grade lethargy over a long period of time, or it can emerge quickly following a traumatic event or even out of the blue. It is a phenomenon that can be observable to others, or it can be hidden by the individual experiencing the pain. Anyone who thinks she may be experiencing depression should be aware of the signs and symptoms. Untreated depression can lead to suicidal thought and potentially to self-harm and even completed suicide. Although depression is not always progressive when it is untreated, some risk remains that it will progress. With treatment, depression has an extremely high rate for a successful recovery to full functioning. Therefore, it is important to know the signs of depression and use the resources noted in this chapter if the described symptoms match what is being experienced.

One of the common symptoms of depression is feeling hopeless. Feelings of hopelessness can be described as not believing that anything good will happen or that life has positive experiences in store for the future. Hopelessness can be a pervasive feeling that affects relationships, work, friendships, and the desire to engage in activities. The person feeling hopeless may ask himself, "What's the point?" This person may lose interest in all the activities that he once enjoyed and begin to isolate himself from friends and family. Feelings of hopelessness can affect all levels of the individual's ability to function, as well as important relationships. The hopeless person may feel that life is just not worth living.

Another common symptom of depression is a significant change in sleep patterns and eating habits. The depressed person may find herself sleeping too much or not being able to fall asleep or stay asleep. Depressed people often find that their thoughts become cyclic at night when they lie down to go to sleep; simple thoughts may circle around and around in the mind and lead to other endless thoughts. The harder that this person tries to fall asleep, the more crowded her mind becomes with thoughts. Nighttime can become torturous as she finds herself tossing until the wee hours of the morning. These folks with disrupted sleep must then face the next day already at a disadvantage. They are overtired and still fighting depression. Conversely, others with sleep disruption related to depression may find that they are sleeping endless hours and having difficulty getting out of bed. They may find that all they want to do is sleep and still do not feel rested when they are awake. If someone is either not able to sleep or finds herself sleeping all the time, her daily functioning will be interrupted. This can contribute to an onset of a depressive episode or can increase existing depression.

A significant change in eating habits can be a sign of the onset of depression. Some individuals may experience a dramatic weight loss over a short period of time as they lose their appetite and interest in food. The taste of food can become bland, and the idea of preparing a meal or taking the time to eat can be overwhelming. Others may misinterpret the weight loss as a good thing, particularly in a culture in which being thinner is rewarded. The person who is losing the weight rapidly may not understand that his appetite has decreased because he is depressed. Losing a substantial amount of weight in a short period of time is a signal that something is wrong.

Another change in eating that can be a factor in depression may be a significant increase in weight over a short period of time. This can be caused as the depressed person seeks to self-soothe by eating everything in sight. As the weight increases, the depressed person's physical system becomes slowed, and the depression may be compounded by the additional pounds that she is carrying.

The depressed person may lose ambition and the energy to get to work on time or at all. This individual may find himself crying for no reason at all and may sometimes have difficulty stopping. His concentration and memory can be impaired, and the smallest tasks may seem to take great energy. Depressed individuals may find that they are increasing their use of substances to blunt the emotional pain that they are experiencing. Alcohol and most drugs are depressants, and the increased use of substances can further plunge the person into increased depression.

Depression is an illness that can create disruption in many aspects of someone's life. Important relationships can be affected adversely as the depressed person withdraws from the world. Her spouse or partner and friends may not understand what has happened to the person they once knew to be lively and energized. Interest in sexual activity generally declines as depression increases, and this can create concern or conflict in a relationship. Usual household chores and involvement with the children may decrease and cause further conflict. Those who are closest to the depressed person will be affected the most, and their reactions can further plunge the individual into inertia.

It can be difficult for the depressed person to recognize or admit to himself or others that he may be depressed. Depression is a mental illness that may not be accepted by some, so individuals may try to "pull themselves up by their bootstraps" as they might have been taught to do in childhood. Unfortunately, this does not necessarily work, because depression is often biologically based and may require medical intervention with medication. As much as one may try, sheer willpower may not cure this illness. If someone is experiencing the symptoms noted above, the best thing to do is to talk to a professional. **Depression is treatable. There is hope.**

At times, it is imperative for the depressed person to recognize her symptoms and **get help immediately**. The following symptoms can be warning precursors to suicidal action. Symptoms that require immediate attention include having thoughts about taking one's own life, planning how death can be attempted, giving away belongings, feeling as if death is the only way to solve a problem(s), talking or writing about committing suicide, having the means to commit suicide (weapons, pills), and feeling a need to make out a will or plan one's own funeral. Asking for help may seem to be a daunting task for the depressed person, but it is exactly what she needs to do as soon as she becomes aware that she is experiencing any of these signs of serious mood decline.

Following are the symptoms of depression:

- Hopelessness
- Sleep disruption
- Significant weight gain or loss
- Loss of energy
- Increased substance use
- Impaired concentration and memory
- Crying bouts
- Self-destructive thoughts
- Poor sense of self
- Negative thinking
- Isolation
- Moodiness
- Always feeling run down

The following symptoms indicate that a person's depression has increased in severity:

- Giving away possessions and favorite objects
- Talking about death and dying
- Feeling suicidal
- Preoccupation with wills and insurance
- Becoming unusually violent or taking dangerous risks
- Talking or writing about suicide

The following symptoms of depression require immediate intervention:

- When someone states that he or she is going to commit suicide
- When someone has a plan of how he or she will commit suicide
- When someone has suicidal thoughts and access to the means to commit suicide (weapons, drugs)

▦ When Someone You Love Needs Help

Many signs and symptoms help to identify someone who may be experiencing suicidal thought and feelings. Some of these signs may be easily recognizable, while others are cloaked and often invisible to the observer. Observable signs for concern can include many changes in behavior. One of these behavioral changes could be a disruption in sleep patterns. When an individual is depressed, he may sleep too much because he does not have the will or energy to get out of bed. Sleep patterns that are also affected by depression may include the inability to sleep, trouble falling asleep, and trouble staying asleep. Significant changes in eating routines can also be an observable sign of depression. Some individuals who are depressed simply lose their appetite, and weight loss can occur quickly and dramatically, or over time. Other people who are depressed may attempt to soothe themselves with food and may eat much more than they have in the past. Significant weight gain or weight loss can be an indicator that something is wrong.

Another observable sign that a loved one may be experiencing depression is their being moodier or unhappier than usual. This may show itself in episodes of crying, withdrawal from others and isolating herself, and irritability. Any major change in mood or difference in personality may be a sign that the individual is experiencing emotional issues that need attention. This is especially true if the mood change is dramatic or continues over a period of time. Everyone has times when they feel unhappy or frustrated; the distinction with someone who is depressed is that these periods of moodiness are not fleeting, and they may be disruptive to the individual's daily functioning or to those around them.

Individuals experiencing depression may appear to be run down and lacking the energy to do the things that they once enjoyed. Usual activities that may have once brought pleasure and interest no longer have any appeal to the depressed person. This individual may isolate and appear withdrawn and tired. Hobbies, physical activity, sexual interest, and other once-enjoyable pastimes require more energy than the depressed person can muster.

An increase in the use of substances can be an observable sign that someone is depressed. Self-medication with chemicals, including alcohol and drugs, initially may help the depressed person mask feelings of sadness and hopelessness. Paradoxically, many of these substances are also depressants and can further plunge the person into a major depression. Compounding this, substance use can distort thinking and increase impulsivity that can lead to an act of self-harm. Depression and the use of substances can be a lethal combination.

Other observable signs that someone may be depressed or suicidal include beginning to give away personal items or showing an unusual interest in wills, funerals, or insurance policies. If a loved one talks about suicide or wanting to die or states that she doesn't have anything to live for anymore, the concerned person needs to take action.

He can encourage his loved one to call a counselor or hotline. If the loved one will not make the call, the concerned person can make the call to the hotline himself to ask what he can do next. The concerned person should not take on the role of giving advice or trying to solve the other person's problems. These circumstances are best managed by a professional, who can see the situation objectively.

■ Resources

External resources for help can be within an arm's reach for the suicidal person. Family members and friends can play a crucial role in the recovery of the suicidal individual by picking up cues that their loved one is distressed. As stated, clues that can indicate that someone may be depressed or suicidal can include seeing changes in the distressed person's behavior, such as sleeping or eating more or less than usual. Other clues might be a change in weight, appearance, or mood; hearing direct or indirect statements about wishing to be dead; or seeing evidence of the distressed person giving away belongings or having a preoccupation with death. Some suicidal individuals may not be able to ask for help for a multitude of reasons. They may fear that they will not be understood or believed, they may fear that they will be "put away," or they may be so depressed that they cannot communicate what they are experiencing to another. Family members, friends, and co-workers are often the first people to observe signs that someone they are close to is in trouble. A concerned other can then follow up by asking the distressed person questions, listening to her, taking her seriously, and facilitating a referral to a professional. If there is ever any question that the distressed individual is in imminent danger of self-harm, it is imperative that concerned others call 9-1-1 immediately.

If the suicidal individual is able to reach out and ask for help, it is vital that the person receiving the information take it seriously. Help may be requested of family members and friends in an indirect and ambiguous fashion, such as the individual stating that he "doesn't have much to live for anymore" or "it would be better if I weren't around." The untrained family member or friend may not understand that this could be an opening to begin a conversation with the distressed person about getting help. Additionally, the untrained person may hope that this is a fleeting feeling for the loved one and fear that talking about it openly will increase the feelings of suicide. Important others need to know that talking about suicide cannot cause suicide; in fact, talking about suicide can sometimes begin the process of recovery. When the suicidal person knows that he is being taken seriously and feels understood, he may be willing to take the next step and see a professional.

Unfortunately, as hard as it may be for the suicidal person to ask for assistance, she may have to do so more than once and in a more direct fashion. If she is not taken seriously or her feelings are minimized when she first requests help, the suicidal person may need to seek assistance from more than one person. Requesting help can require a Herculean effort from the depressed person, who may be experiencing lethargy and have diminished energy. It is important for the distressed individual to remember, however, that it takes only one person to listen and understand to help decrease her isolation and begin the process of getting help. The suicidal person needs to keep talking until someone listens and takes seriously what she is saying. Family members and friends need to trust their instincts and not hope that their loved one is in a phase that will pass. Important others need to be direct if concerned, ask questions, and offer to help with setting up appointments with a counselor. A life may be saved by the validation and support of a concerned family member or friend.

The more isolated suicidal person may not have a close-knit group of family members or friends that he can talk to or who may notice when there are dramatic changes in his behavior. This isolation can be especially dangerous and add to the suicidal individual's feelings of loneliness and depression. These people may have contact with others only at the workplace or school environment, where they may be even less likely to disclose their feelings of distress. Resources exist for these individuals in the form of direct contact with any number of community organizations, which include their local mental health clinic, the National Suicide Prevention hotline, and any local individual counselor. Contact can be initiated with the local mental health clinic or a private counselor through a phone directory under the heading "Counselors." The direct number for the National Suicide Prevention hotline is 1-800-273-TALK (8255). This number will route any national call to a hotline nearest the caller and to a person who is available to listen and provide information and referrals 24 hours a day, seven days a week. Other community resources include religious leaders, primary health care providers, support groups, and law enforcement. The same resources can be used by family members and friends if they have concerns about a loved one being suicidal and don't know what to do. Hotlines are staffed by individuals who are trained to know how to help both the person who is feeling thoughts of self-harm and the concerned others who may not know how to assist their loved one.

■ Strategies for the Suicidal Person

The single most important strategy for the suicidal person in her recovery is to recognize her feelings and to talk about them with a trusted other. The suicidal person may be experiencing feelings of hopelessness and hold the belief that nothing will help, and thus reaching out can require tremendous effort. This effort to reach out may be the first and one of the most crucial steps in her recovery. Once the suicidal individual has disclosed her feelings, she will no longer be alone with her distress. If she has chosen to talk to a family member or friend, this trusted person can assist her in reaching out to a mental health professional. If the suicidal person has directly called a suicide hotline or counselor, the professional will work to get her connected to resources that can facilitate her healing.

The suicidal person must know that help is available and that depression is a treatable illness. Specific thoughts, feelings, and behaviors indicate that someone should get help right away. These may include the wish to die, thinking about ways to die and making a plan, giving away possessions, believing that death is the only way to solve problems, losing interest in usual activities, and engaging in risky behaviors. If someone is experiencing these feelings or demonstrating these behaviors, he should reach out immediately to a family member, a friend, or one of the community resources noted above and at the end of this chapter. At times, suicidal individuals may feel that suicidal thought is a sign of weakness and that they should be able to handle their problems on their own. Suicidal thought is usually a symptom of depression and not anyone's fault; it does not have to be dealt with alone and, in fact, is best managed with a professional. The suicidal person should know that counseling and medicine can help. In fact, the prognosis for depression and for people with suicidal thought is excellent when treated with both therapy and medication. With treatment, the symptoms of depression that include suicidality can disappear. There is hope.

The suicidal person may not know what to say when she first speaks with a concerned other or picks up the telephone to call a counselor. The best strategy is to use words that are honest to describe feelings and behaviors. For example, "I have not been feeling like there is any point to living anymore"; or, "I don't feel like eating, and all I want to do is sleep"; or, "Sometimes I wish I didn't have to wake up." If the suicidal person is speaking with an untrained friend or family member, he may not understand the seriousness of the conversation, so it may be necessary for the suicidal person to find someone who truly understands and talk to that person.

If you are feeling suicidal, take the following action:

- Call a professional (listed under "Counselors' in the local phone directory).
- Call the local or national hotline (1-800-273-TALK) anytime day, night, or weekend.
- Talk to a trusted other (friend, family member, church leader, health care worker). Use clear, direct words, such as "I don't feel like living anymore and I think I need help."
- Talk to another trusted person if you do not feel understood the first time you reach out.
- Keep talking until you find someone who listens and understands.
- Know that depression is treatable and recovery rates are quite high.

▨ Strategies for the Concerned Other

The importance of family members and friends cannot be minimized, and this can be especially true when there is a loved one who has suicidal predisposition. Family and friends are the people who are on the frontline in the distressed person's battle against depression. They are often the first to observe changes in behaviors and mood, and are often the first to intervene.

When a family member or friend intervenes with a suicidal person, his strategies should include nonjudgmental listening, gentle questions, and facilitating a referral to a professional. There may be some tendency on the part of concerned others to minimize what they are seeing and hearing. Although these minimization impulses may be part of the human defense system and a way to block out the pain of someone who is loved, it is necessary to act on what is heard and not just hope that it will change. Tomorrow the loved one may not feel better, and, in fact, the depression could deepen if untreated. While it is never a concerned person's responsibility if someone completes suicide, he can have some impact to change the outcome.

The first and most important response a concerned other can have with the suicidal person is to take her seriously. It is critical not to judge her or wonder if she is "just seeking attention." If someone makes a suicidal statement, it is, indeed, a cry for help and professional attention is the best intervention to truly determine if there is a possibility of self-harm. Concerned others are not objective and may have difficulty believing that someone they care about could be in enough despair to take her own life. While a concerned other may hope that a loved one's mood will change, this is not always the case. If the concerned person does not know what to say or how to intervene with the suicidal individual, she can call the hotline noted above and at the end of this section. The trained hotline staff will coach her in how to best proceed.

If there is ever any threat of imminent harm, the police should be called right away. For example, if someone says, "I have a gun, and I am going to kill myself," it is time to immediately call 9-1-1. It is not the role of the concerned person to try to wrestle a weapon away from someone or to hope that the person in despair doesn't really have a gun and is just blowing off steam. The concerned person may have the mistaken assumption that he has the relationship power to convince the family member or friend that she has too much too live for to kill herself. The suicidal person may feel enough pressure from her concerned other in that moment to stop her suicide attempt. However, without professional help, the underlying source of the pain will not be dealt with, and the suicidal impulse may resurface. Therefore, when there is any indication that someone has a plan and intent to kill herself, a professional should be called immediately.

It is also important that concerned others do not take on too much sole responsibility for keeping their loved ones safe from self-harm. This can be a monumental task if a person is intent on killing himself and can take a toll on concerned others. If a concerned person finds herself worrying all the time, continually checking to see if the loved one is "okay," or notices the signs and symptoms of depression that are listed in this chapter, she should call a professional counselor or the hotline to talk. Dealing with a suicidal person is too much to responsibility to carry alone. Caring about others is a wonderful thing, but at times this caring should translate into getting a professional involved. The professional is trained to help the concerned other with her concerns and to coach the concerned person in how to navigate the tumultuous waters that surround a suicidal person.

In less immediate circumstances, if a concerned person is worried about a loved one, there are questions to ask and words to say that can guide the suicidal person toward professional help. The concerned person sometimes believes that he can make a person suicidal if he raises the question about suicide. This is not the case. As stated previously, the only person responsible for a completed suicide is the suicidal person herself. Many times the suicidal person will experience a feeling of relief that she is understood and cared about when a concerned other asks questions.

Much like the suicidal person who may not know how to disclose feelings of suicidality, the concerned other may not know how to approach the person she is worried about. The best manner in which to talk to the suicidal person is to be caring and direct. For example, the concerned person could ask, "You have seemed down for a long time, and I've been worried about you. Have you had any thoughts about ending your own life?" Or, the concerned other may ask, "I have been thinking about you, and you don't seem to be yourself. You're sleeping all the time and just don't appear happy. Have you had any thoughts about suicide?"

These questions can be hard for the concerned person to ask but are important for many reasons. If the loved one is indeed suicidal and can admit it, then the journey toward healing has begun. If the loved one is suicidal but is unable to say so, a seed will be planted for her that may later give her permission to go to the concerned other with her feelings. The concerned person may have to ask more than once if he remains worried and if the signs and symptoms of depression continue. The questions about suicide provide information, create an indication that someone notices and cares, and can begin a process for the individual to get help.

Once the suicidal person is able to disclose that he has had suicidal thoughts, the concerned person can facilitate the helping process. A wonderful follow-up statement to the suicidal person could be, "I can hear that you are really hurting. Let me call this number for you, and after you make an appointment to talk to someone, I would be happy to go with you if you would like." Sometimes the person with suicidal thoughts may not be ready to make an appointment to talk with a professional. This can be hard for the concerned person, who wants assurance that her loved one will get help. It is good to understand that the first time an appointment is suggested, it is often declined. However, the seed has been planted that help is available; the hurting person will remember this and may use the resources provided to him at another time. If the person with suicidal thoughts and feelings is unwilling to get help but is not at immediate risk, there is no need to panic or call 9-1-1. The concerned person may be worried or upset enough to call the hotline herself. She may decide to seek her own counseling to manage the anxiety she is feeling as a result of fears regarding a loved one's potential self-harm. If someone has concerns regarding another's ability for self-harm that affect her own daily functioning, she should reach out to any of the described resources for her own help. Suicide is a frightening concept. It needs to be taken seriously, and attention needs to be given not only to the suicidal individual but also to concerned people who are affected by the potential self-destruction of someone they care about.

If you are concerned about someone taking their own life, take the following action:

- Call 9-1-1 if you believe threat of suicide is imminent.
- Listen to and take your loved one seriously.

- Be nonjudgmental.
- Don't be afraid to ask questions such as, "It seems you have been sad for a long time, and I've been wondering if you've had thoughts about killing yourself?"
- Offer to call a professional or a hotline and offer to accompany your loved one to the first appointment.
- Do not take on too much responsibility or become a "counselor."
- Get help for yourself if you find that you are worrying all the time or have questions about how to help your loved one.
- Call 1-800-273-TALK for resources and referrals.

▨ A Basic Recovery Plan for the Suicidal Person

The first step in any recovery plan is to recognize that there is a problem and to be willing to get help for it. This is no different for the depressed and suicidal person. He must be willing to understand that he has a problem and reach out for assistance. Although this may sound simple, it is not. Depression, by its nature, creates difficulty with organization and action. The depressed person may not be able to think through the options that he has and then may not have the energy to follow through. If this person takes an initial step by speaking with a concerned other and then feels misunderstood, he may retreat. Gathering phone numbers to call a professional and then making the calls also takes organization and energy. Some counselors may not be taking on new patients or may not return calls promptly; someone who is depressed can become discouraged easily and may decide not to pursue other counseling options. While this initial step can present hurdles, it is important for the depressed person to remain on his mission and obtain help. He must keep calling until a connection is established with either a concerned other or a professional.

Once the depressed person has made the first call to a hotline or to a counselor, she has set the journey to recovery in place. Most often a connection will be established during the first visit with a counselor, and future visits will be arranged. It is important to know, however, that a first visit with a therapist does not always satisfy the client. The client may not feel heard or understood, or the match between client and counselor may not be a good fit. This is not unusual; it is part of the process of finding the best help that can be found for that particular individual. Having a good connection with a counselor can be of great importance in healing. Meeting one or two therapists and choosing the one who is the best match can be empowering and instrumental in recovery. In the cases in which the first therapist does not feel like a good fit, the client will need to try again with another counselor. She needs to keep trying until she feels she has found a counselor who can understand and help her.

Once a therapeutic relationship with a counselor has been established, the counselor will conduct an assessment of the client to determine the plan for treatment. This assessment may be formal or informal and most likely will consist of the counselor taking a history of the client and asking questions about current symptoms, behaviors, thoughts, and feelings. The therapist may suggest that the client also be evaluated for medication if she thinks this could benefit to the client. While some individuals will not be ready to begin medication, if the counselor recommends an evaluation, it would be a good idea to at least attend the medication assessment session. This session is scheduled with a psychiatric nurse practitioner or a psychiatrist who specializes in mental health medications. The client can think of this evaluation as an information-gathering session. She can listen to the recommendations and think about them, and, if and when she is ready, she will have the knowledge to act. On some occasions, medication will not be recommended.

The counselor that the individual has chosen will work with the client to decide on a treatment plan that may include elements such as cognitive therapy, developing coping strategies, and interpersonal coaching. If the client is actively suicidal and the counselor determines that she may be at risk for self-harm, hospitalization may be recommended or required. If the client has suicidal thoughts but no plan for self-harm, the therapist will work with the client to establish a safety plan.

Each individual's recovery plan will be based on his own particular set of life circumstances and determined by clinician and client together. The therapeutic relationship between client and counselor can become a safe environment in which goals are set. These goals are then worked on until they are met and the depression and suicidal thoughts ease and diminish. The relationship that the patient has with his counselor is a unique and important one. Within the bounds of this relationship, the patient can begin to design a new world that brings him greater comfort and improved functioning in the world.

Coping Strategies

In the therapeutic counseling relationship, coping strategies will be uniquely designed for the specific individual. These strategies will depend on client history and the current thoughts and behaviors of the client. The therapist will work with the client to design strategies that fit her personality and lifestyle; it will be a joint venture into recovery. Each coping strategy will build on the next until the client can step forth into the world ready to manage any relapse she may experience in the future with knowledge and skills.

Universal coping techniques can be utilized by anyone; some of these strategies will be described in the next few paragraphs. The strategies that are discussed in this chapter will include minimizing the use of alcohol or drugs, using positive self-talk, setting healthy boundaries, letting go, exercise, and surrounding oneself with people who are supportive and comforting. These are simple coping strategies and when used in conjunction with therapy, they can help to decrease depression and suicidal thoughts and can improve self-esteem.

Reducing the Use of Substances

Alcohol and drugs are sometimes used by people in distress to self-soothe. It may seem that alcohol, over-the-counter medication, or prescription drugs can relieve distress by helping with sleep, improving socialization, or blunting negative feelings. These positive responses are temporary and fleeting, and do not remove the underlying conditions that may have caused the despair in the first place. Alcohol and over-the-counter medication that is used to assist with sleep can later lead to further sleep disruption. Social impairment may occur when drugs and alcohol are utilized to help someone interact with others. Negative feelings may initially be blunted with the use of substances, but over time, negative feeling can increase rather than decrease. The use of alcohol or drugs can further distort the thinking of someone who may be experiencing depression and can lead to dependence on the substance being used. The paradox is that substance initially may seem to help; however, the reality is that these substances can eventually compound all of the negative effects of the depression that is being masked. The use of alcohol or drugs, including sleeping pills for depression, should be limited unless they are prescribed by a physician.

Positive Self-Talk

Positive self-talk is a simple technique. It is a strategy that begins to change the continual negative chatter that some people repeat to themselves either consciously or unconsciously. Negative thoughts are often automatic and may have begun at a young age. These negative thoughts can be quite engrained in the way in which the person thinks about himself. Many negative self-expressions have originated from a critical caregiver during early childhood and then been adopted by the individual. These negative thoughts are self-defeating and perpetuate and solidify poor self-esteem and depression. Adopting positive self-talk can be a difficult coping strategy to implement for people who have a poor sense of self or who are feeling depressed. These individuals may not believe that there is anything good about them; thus, using positive language may seem untruthful to them. They can begin with a simple mantra, "I am okay just the way I am." While these people may not believe that they are "okay" in the beginning, the more they replace a negative thought with a positive thought, the more this belief will become solidified. Negative thoughts have been engrained and repeated for years; the replacement of them will take time and the belief about the positive will follow.

Changing negative self-talk requires three basic steps. The first step is to notice the negative thought; these thoughts are automatic and can be subtle. Once the thought has been identified, the individual needs to mindfully and gently push the thought aside, which is the second step. The last step is to replace the negative thought with a positive thought. This process may sound easy, but the negative thoughts probably have become entrenched after many years of repetition. They can be changed, but it requires diligence and practice. As stated, some individuals think they cannot replace the negative thought with a positive one because they do not believe the positive affirmation. For example, replacing "I am attractive" for the long-repeated negative thought "I am ugly" may feel dishonest for those who have become conditioned to truly believe they are unattractive. Repeating these words, even if they are not believed at first, eventually will lead to a shift in core feelings about the self. Using positive self-talk can require a leap of faith; the process will work if it is practiced. The negative self-beliefs will change if the positive replacement thoughts continue, but this process requires time and patience.

Setting Boundaries

Setting healthy boundaries is an excellent coping skill to develop. Some people have never learned to say no and, therefore, they spend their lives feeling overwhelmed and underappreciated. Setting a boundary for the first time can require considerable emotional energy, but it does become easier over time. The reward for setting a boundary is generally immediate. For example, when a task is refused, then the time is freed up for something else. This positive reinforcement can be powerful and help to provide incentive for setting further boundaries. Having healthy boundaries is a way to develop and preserve a strong sense of self. It is a healthy way in which one protects one's personal space and the space of others.

For individuals who need to develop boundaries, a good place to begin may be in reducing the time and effort spent with or on abusive or neglectful others. People with poor self-esteem often allow others who can be physically or emotionally abusive to control their lives. Setting boundaries with the time that is spent with these difficult others can be achieved slowly so that it does not feel overwhelming or frightening to the person setting the boundary. Begin setting a boundary by letting the telephone machine pick up messages and screen calls. Return only the calls that are received from someone who is caring and gives back emotional support. Surround oneself with caring others instead of those who are always making requests or who are belittling. Setting boundaries is another skill that takes time to develop, and the support of a counselor can be especially helpful in addressing the issues that arise as one learns this strategy.

It can be helpful to begin to set boundaries by saying "no." Saying no can seem to be impossible to someone who has always set out to please others. When there is no ability to be discerning and someone is always accommodating to everyone else, resentment will build. The pleaser finds himself with little or no time for himself. He also may feel as if everyone else depends on him and that he never has people reach out to support him. What the person with no boundaries must remember is that others cannot read his mind. When someone asks for a favor and the response is affirmative, the person who has asked for the favor assumes that everything is fine. This person cannot know that the pleaser is fuming inside and does not want to provide the service that has been requested. It is up to the individual to set clear boundaries and say no if he does not want to accommodate the request. The first few times that someone takes the risk to say no can be frightening. He may fear that others will be angry at him or that he will be abandoned. Remarkably, when someone gathers up the courage to say, "I just can't do that right now," he often finds that others understand. In setting boundaries and learning to say "no," it can be helpful to develop a handful of brief responses or sound bites to use when others make requests.

Examples of these sound bites include the following:

- "I'm sorry; I'm really tied up for the next week."
- "I wish I could help, but I have too much on my own plate right now."
- "It sounds like it could be fun, but I have other plans for the weekend."
- "I prefer to spend some time alone."

Brief responses without too much explanation are heard better by others. When justifications are added or the individual feels as if she needs to provide a detailed series of reasons that she is saying no, the message can be lost. Try to stick with a short sentence and then if the other person continues to press, use another variation of the brief response, such as, "I just can't; I have too much to do." Keep it short and sweet. A boundary has then been set.

In the aftermath of setting boundaries for the first time, the individual may experience feelings of guilt. These feelings are normal, and it is important not to react to them. Once the boundary has been set, the hardest part of the work has been completed. Notice the feelings of guilt and hold the boundary. As boundaries become more familiar and are set more frequently, the feelings of guilt will diminish. Setting boundaries is a healthy practice and a wonderful coping skill during times of stress. While coping skills are more easily developed and practiced when life is at its best, they can be learned and utilized at any time.

Letting Go

Letting go is a coping skill that can be developed over time. To be able to let go is a learning process. Every small step that can be taken to let go of emotional baggage will make the journey of life lighter. Some individuals fear that to let go means to stop caring; this is not so. Letting go means to care deeply and understand that control of external circumstances is not possible. One cannot control what happened in the past, but one can work to let go of the anger and resentment that they may carry. The reality is that there is little ability to hold true control over other people, situations, and outcomes. Once a person can let go of the idea that he can have control over others and their environment, the focus can be turned inward. Once the focus is turned inward, toward the self, rather than others, true change is possible. As the focus shifts from the external to the internal, it enables each person to work on himself and address his own life instead of trying to change everything else. Letting go provides freedom for a deeper love of self and others.

It is much easier to look at the external world and others and hope that they will change so that things can improve. It is much more difficult for the individual to focus on what she might do to make her life better. Letting go of expectations for others requires practice and self-talk. In addition to letting go of the expectations that are held for others, it is important to begin to let go of issues in the past that cannot be changed. To ruminate on an incident from the past or an upcoming event does not change the fact that the event occurred or change the outcome of the upcoming situation. The only purpose the rumination has is to distance oneself from the present moment and the experiences that one could be having. Letting go of ruminations, like the other coping skills discussed, requires practice. Human beings are skilled at worrying about what has just happened, what happened 10 years ago, and what could happen next week. While there may never be a complete freedom from worry about what has passed or what is to come, with practice, the worry can be minimized. As with many of the other coping skills, self-talk is crucial. Once rumination or worry is noticed, the individual needs to gently remind herself that she does not need to think about the issue right now. She needs to guide herself back to the here and now. The thoughts may creep back in, and, once again, as soon as they are noticed, they must be gently pushed away. Over time, the thoughts will space themselves out and the individual will find herself more often in the present moment. Rather than agonizing about what has passed, what is to come, and what others are doing, the focus turns inward. This is the only true place for change.

Other Skills

Other basic coping skills include correcting sleep patterns, eating correctly, exercising, self-soothing (hot baths, special tea, beach walks, music), and surrounding oneself with loving family and friends. Keeping to a routine is also an important way to maintain consistency and expectation.

Medical intervention may be necessary to assist with some of the strategies. For example, sleep disruption may be biologically based and require medication to improve the sleep cycle. Medication may be necessary to assist with needed improvement in energy to invest in building coping skills. While some of the coping skills can be mastered without medication, the work to learn and practice the skills is much easier with medication when it is warranted.

■ Finding New Meaning

The depressed and suicidal person may have a worldview that has been filled with despair and hopelessness. He may have wondered whether life is worth living and may have contemplated suicide. As this person begins to reach out to concerned others and can see a glimmer of hope, a small shift is created. Therapy, surrounding oneself with loving others, medication, and coping skills can combine to create a new way of being in the world for the person who once wanted to die.

Separately, each of these resources can have some impact on the depressed person; combined, they are formidable tools in the battle against depression. The prognosis for an individual with depression and suicidal thought who is treated with therapy and medication is excellent. The medication addresses the biological needs of the individual while the therapy works to build cognitive skills, coping skills, and positive interpersonal relationships. New meaning will be cocreated between therapist and client, and the client will rejoin the world with a new outlook. As the individual reemerges from his depression, he will see the world through a different lens and can design his life plan in any new way he desires. He will have learned the skills and resources to deal with depression if it should return; he will have a new hope instilled in him that life can be a happier experience for him.

5 ▪ ▪ ▪

Surviving a Loved One's Suicide

▪ Case Example: The Survivor

Richard had always known that someday he would hear the news. He just knew it, deep inside him. There had been something very different about his mentor for many years; he was not the same person who had taken Richard under his wing when he was a young boy and coached him through all the difficult times in his life. Richard had grown up without much parental support in his young life. His mother had been an alcoholic who drank a fifth of vodka every day, and his father had not been around much; as a youngster, Richard would walk the streets and felt as if it was unsafe to go home. When he met his mentor at church, Richard was starving for someone to look up to and believe in. His mentor would listen to him for hours at a time, providing the first experience Richard had ever had with a consistent, loving adult. These talks went on for years and provided Richard with a sense of self and direction. Richard's words about his mentor were that "he saved me when I was a kid." His mentor had encouraged Richard to attend college and earn a degree. As he got older, his relationship with his mentor had naturally changed to a more equalized friendship. Richard and his mentor had continued to spend time together, and at one point, they in the same apartment complex. His mentor had married, and a few years later Richard married as well.

Throughout the years, Richard slowly began to notice that things seemed to have changed between his mentor and the world. His mentor was drinking alcohol and smoking marijuana on a daily basis and seemed to become judgmental and even paranoid at times. The discussions that they used to have that had been so comforting and easy changed to disagreements, and eventually Richard and his mentor had a falling out. Richard kept tabs on his mentor but had no contact with him; at one point, he had spoken to another friend about how sure he was that his mentor was going to take his own life. Richard had wondered whether he should try to intervene. He had been encouraged not to do so, because there had been some concern about his mentor's level of violence and Richard's safety.

Richard recalls that exactly 10 days after his conversation with this friend, he received a call telling him his mentor was dead from completed suicide. Richard reports that he had hoped that he was wrong about his mentor being suicidal but that he was not surprised about the death. He reports that he felt tremendous guilt for not trying to meet with his mentor and talk to him about his concerns that he would kill himself. Richard also states that he believes that if he had tried to talk to his mentor, he might also be dead now, as well.

Richard describes spending the next six months looking out the window. "My life stopped. I was in shock." Richard developed stomach pains from clenching his stomach continually and felt cold all the time. He felt like he could not get warm. He would walk and walk, as he had when he was a child, with no destination. Richard did start counseling but did not find it helpful to him. He was looking for a way to feel better, to forgive himself and his mentor. He took part in a "rebirthing process," which felt traumatic to him and increased his feelings of vulnerability instead of helping him recover. One day, almost six months after the suicide, Richard reports he woke up and threw everything in the house out the window, both things that belonged to his mentor and to him. He felt this was a cleansing experience for him and finally began the road to his recovery.

Richard's wife was supportive, and he felt that he wouldn't have survived the pain of the suicide without her support. He also states that he was not truly sure he would survive himself until approximately eight months after the death of his mentor when he had had a dream. In the dream, he met his mentor in a bar that they had frequented. His mentor looked strange, and Richard asked him what was wrong. His mentor replied that he was sad because he had to leave him; in this dream Richard responded that nothing his mentor could do would change the way Richard felt about him. This dream was cathartic for Richard and helped him to move forward.

Richard describes feeling suicidal himself until the dream. He reports that the most helpful thing for him during the initial period following the suicide was to be around people who were supportive and who would listen to him. Richard reports that he spoke openly about his feelings and that this was helpful to him. He also states that he didn't want to kill himself because he didn't want to do what his mentor had done to anyone else. He knew that his wife wanted him to stay with her and that others cared, and he did not want to hurt them.

Richard states that slowly the cold went away and his body began to feel warm again. He describes his mentor as still holding a powerful place in his life. Richard wants other survivors to know that the best thing that they can do is to surround themselves with positive people. "No good will come from negativity." Richard offers encouraging words and hope to other survivors. He believes that time helps to heal and that seeking help from others can provide solace in the darkest hours.

▨ Those Left Behind: Surviving the Loss of a Family Member or Friend

Losing a loved one to death can be a life-altering experience. Losing a loved one to death by suicide can profoundly change the way surviving family and friends view the world. Acquaintances can also be affected by suicide in a way that is life altering.

Death is a mysterious and often-feared phenomenon in this culture. When someone dies though illness or the tragedy of sudden accident, those left behind have endless questions. Why did my friend have to be struck down so suddenly? Why was she in that specific place at the specific time of that accident? Why did my loved one die from cancer? Why could he not have been one of the people to be cured when so many others recover? Why does my child, of all children, have to be diagnosed with a fatal illness? Where is God? How can God allow this person I love so deeply to suffer and die? The depth of despair that each of us must face when we lose a parent, a friend, a beloved family member, or a child to the mystery of death is no small matter. Beliefs about the universe, our belief system, and our spirituality are challenged. Our own individual vulnerabilities are raised as we witness death. We are reminded that our own lives are terminal and have a finite ending.

Facing the death of a loved one who has made the choice to take his own life can be dumbfounding. It is not in most people's worldview to understand suicide or the depth of despair a suicidal person may be feeling. It also is difficult to comprehend that a person who has made the decision to end his life may be making a conscious choice that is not the result of extreme despair, but rather simply a decision not to live in this world. How do those who remain make sense of what can appear to be such a senseless act? Our personal beliefs are stretched, and our minds cannot comprehend such a radical choice. The grieving for the loss of someone by suicide is extraordinarily complicated. There is the original grief from loss, which is then compounded by additional layers of confusion, anger, guilt, and feelings of powerlessness.

There are 30,000 deaths by suicide each year in the United States. The number of people significantly affected by these deaths can be up to and beyond 300,000 individuals. If a family member, friend, or colleague has died by suicide, many other survivors are suffering the same kind of loss and wrestling with the same deep questions. Why? Could I have done anything to prevent the suicide? How could this have happened?

There are many questions. Some of the inevitable questions may never be answered, and living without answers and the ambiguity of the loss can feel insurmountable at first. How does the survivor of a loved one's suicide go on living?

Every survivor of a loved one's death by suicide is different; therefore, each will have his own unique responses and time frame regarding the loss. Some of the reactions will seem to be universal, and some will be specific to the survivor's history and personal life story. The path of recovery can depend on the survivor's internal resiliency, coping skills, and supports. However, coping skills can be learned, supports can be expanded, and resiliency can be developed. The ones left behind have a journey to take that can be filled with pain, emotion, and, in time, recovery. Some sense of loss and questions about the suicide may always remain, but the survivor who has recovered will be able to function in the world with a sense of peace and closure.

Survivors reading about recovery for the first time may have their doubts that they will ever have peace of mind. Recovery is a process, and although there may always be a feeling of loss for the deceased, the raw emotion will lessen with time.

■ Stages and Reactions to Loss

Elisabeth Kubler-Ross describes five stages of grief. She applied her work to any form of catastrophic personal loss such as job, income, divorce, and the death of a loved one. Kubler-Ross believed that the steps of grief do not necessarily follow in a straightforward order, and some of the steps may not be experienced by all who experience grief. Rather, the steps act as a guide to understand a universal process of loss. Each of the stages offer an opportunity to work through grief, and each survivor of catastrophic loss such as suicide will make her way through the stages at her own pace and in her own order.

The initial stage described by Kubler-Ross is one of denial. Survivors' first response to the news that a loved one has died by suicide may be disbelief and a feeling that this simply could not be true. They may experience an out-of-body sensation and a feeling of unreality, like trying to move through waves in the ocean. The moment of receiving such tragic news can appear to be locked in time. Survivors may feel that this just cannot be happening to them or be real. They may want to return in time to the previous moment or day. Everything slows down or appears to move too fast. Survivors may experience a sense of shock. Numbness, disorientation, and trouble concentrating are common features in the first few moments and days after receiving the news. Survivors may struggle to understand how this could be possible and why their loved one would take his own life. They may find themselves asking "why?" many times, especially if they didn't see any warning signs of suicidal intent.

If a survivor was the one to find the body of the deceased loved one following a suicide, other symptoms she experiences can be considered severe and ultimately could create post-traumatic stress syndrome or acute stress disorder in the survivor. Post-traumatic stress syndrome and acute stress disorder have features that include nightmares; intrusive, disturbing thoughts and memories about the scene of the suicide; impaired concentration and memory; disrupted sleep and eating habits; avoidance of any reminders of the suicide; impairment in daily functioning; depersonalization; and dissociative amnesia (inability to remember the scene or specific details of the event). Some of these severe symptoms may be experienced by the survivor who has not witnessed the suicide scene. In either case, if a survivor is having adverse reactions that affect her daily functioning, she should seek professional help.

The suicide survivor may next experience deep sadness and loss that may be accompanied by crying, wailing, and deep emotional pain. This is all a normal part of grief. Kubler-Ross notes that the second step in grieving is anger, which can accompany the feelings of deep sadness and loss. The survivor may feel rage that his loved one could leave him behind to carry the burden. He may wonder how his friend or family member could do something so selfish and that hurts him so much. This anger may be powerful, and the survivor may experience guilt for having this feeling and try to push the anger aside. Anger is a normal response to a loved one's self-destruction. It is one of a multitude of feelings that the survivor can experience off and on throughout the healing process. The anger may be directed at the person who committed suicide; it also can be self-directed. Self-directed anger can be the result of the belief that the survivor did not do enough to stop the suicide. This self-directed anger is closely related to guilt. Some survivors may blame themselves for not doing more to stop the loved one's suicide. They feel guilt at themselves for not making one more phone call or seeing one more sign that their friend or family member was about to commit suicide. They may agonize about the last time that they saw their loved one alive, replaying everything they did and said. They may be angry and guilty that they did not do more, say more, and act more aggressively to get help for the person they care about so deeply and who is now gone forever. While self-directed anger may be part of the grieving process, it is important for the survivor to remember that if his loved one truly intended to die, there is nothing he could have done to stop it. It is also impossible to predict the future behavior of another; therefore, knowing that someone had the true intent to commit suicide at any specific moment in time is not a realistic possibility.

Anger may be directed at another person such as a therapist or someone else close to the person who completed suicide. The anger may appear to be rational anger at times, and at other moments, the rage may feel explosive and out of control, for no objective reason. This anger is part of the process of grief. It can be most helpful to wait to take any action until time has passed and thoughts and emotions are more stable. In the midst of the grief process, thinking may not be at its best as the flood of feelings masks rational thought.

Kubler-Ross describes the third stage of grieving as that of bargaining. Bargaining is a stage, generally before a person dies, in which the individual barters with the universe to help a loved one recover. For example, she may plead with God to allow her terminally ill child to live and to take her own life instead. Bargaining generally is not experienced by the suicide survivor because the loved one has already passed away. A reaction in the grieving process, which is not in Kubler-Ross's model, that can be felt by the suicide survivor is that of experiencing relief. Some suicidal people suffer for a long time with a difficult mental illness. It can become clear to concerned others that their loved one really did not want to live and that their prolonged life was not one in which they experienced any happiness. There may have been previous multiple suicide attempts or hospitalizations. Thus, the suicide can be experienced by the survivor as a relief that his loved one's suffering has finally ended. As with anger, the feeling of relief may be complicated by accompanying feelings of guilt. The survivor may shame himself and feel guilt for being glad that the ordeal of watching the family member or friend in pain is over. It will be helpful for the survivor to remember that all feelings are normal, especially following a traumatic event. The feeling of relief is a human response. And, indeed, the reality is that the suffering of some who have died by suicide will be ended.

The fourth stage in Kubler-Ross's model of grieving is that of depression. The survivor may experience many symptoms of depression to varying degrees. These symptoms can include lethargy, poor concentration, sleep and appetite disturbance, memory impairment, extreme moodiness, anger and irritability, prolonged crying spells, and disruption of daily functioning. The survivor may experience suicidal feelings herself and wonder whether she can go on without her loved one. The survivor should obtain help for herself if she experiences suicidal thoughts or if the symptoms of depression persist and affect her daily life functioning. Depression can be consuming, and, as we have seen from earlier chapters, reaching out for help is the best way to combat this painful response to a loved one's suicide.

The final stage of the grief process, according to Kubler-Ross's model, is that of acceptance. The suicide survivor may never completely accept that he has lost his loved one to suicide, but eventually he can reach a place in his healing when he can acknowledge that it is going to be okay. The survivor will come to realize that he can go on, even without all the answers that he wants. He will have navigated his way through the initial roller coaster of emotions, and, while he may still have feelings of loss, these feelings will no longer be overwhelming.

■ The Complicated Grief of the Suicide Survivor

The grief of the suicide survivor is complicated and differs from other bereavement in several ways. This grief can be prolonged as the survivor searches for motives and faces questions about the circumstances of their loved one's death. Many times the survivor has difficulty coming to terms with or believing that the death was by suicide. In fact, a death may be ruled an accident or a homicide, and still there may be questions about suicide. Conversely, the death can be determined legally to be a suicide, but questions may remain regarding whether there was an accident or murder. The questions surrounding suicide can linger and may never be resolved completely. For some survivors, the ambiguity surrounding their loved one's death may be especially painful and a quest for answers can go on indefinitely.

Lawrence Calhoun and B. Allen note that survivors of suicidal deaths may view others as being less supportive and more rejecting of them than individuals who are coping with deaths from other events such as illness or accident. They also note that suicide survivors may experience the same type of social stigma that is carried by the act of suicide. They go on to state that survivors of suicide are regarded by others as "more psychologically disturbed, less likable, more blameworthy, more ashamed, more in need of professional mental health care and more likely to remain sad and depressed longer." The nature of a death by suicide not only leaves the survivor with many questions about the death itself, but also may bring up questions about his potential role in the loss. He may feel self-recrimination, guilt, and shame. The survivor may believe that others around him blame him and wonder why he did not do more to help his friend or relative. These feelings of blame can lead the survivor to isolate himself and deepen his feelings of guilt. The survivor may feel pressure to explain to others what happened to his loved one and why it occurred. He may feel backed into a corner by questions he cannot answer and may lie or avoid talking about the means of death because it is so shameful or painful.

Survivor grief can be complicated as those left behind must also manage any feelings of rejection that they have after being left by the person who completed suicide. A spouse may wonder how her partner could have left her to deal with the children, the bills, and all the other parts of the life that they had shared. Feelings of rejection and anger may intertwine with other feelings of sadness and guilt. Some partners may believe that if they were more lovable, their spouse would not have committed suicide. Questions such as "how could he have left me alone?" may become a mantra that has no answer. As difficult as it may be, it is important for the survivor to understand that the person who was in such pain that he needed to take his own life was focused inward. He could not see any way past his own despair, and his action was no reflection on his feelings for the others in his life. In fact, some individuals who complete suicide may believe that they are a burden to their loved ones and that their act of suicide is a way that they can help ease their family members' travails.

A child survivor of a parent's suicide may experience feelings of deep rejection and loss. These emotions can manifest themselves in different ways throughout the child's developmental life cycle. As a young child, the feeling of terror at being left behind in the world may be predominant, along with feelings of sadness. However, these emotions may change to rage or depression in later years and may be combined with the use of substances to self-medicate from feelings of being abandoned and rejected. Some children may experience self-blame for not being "good enough" for their parent to stay with them or feel that in some way they were the cause of their parent's suicide. The child may believe that if he had had earned better grades, not spoken back, or kept his room clean, the parent would still be alive. If the last interaction that the child had with the loved one was negative, the child may take on the full responsibility for the death of the adult. Recovery from these beliefs and feelings can be a long and painful process, and symptoms may manifest in a variety of forms throughout the life cycle. Some children may experience anxiety that other loved ones will also leave them and can develop feelings of abandonment as a key life issue that affects all their relationships. While a child who loses a loved one for any reason may experience a sense of being abandoned, the loss of someone to suicide can magnify abandonment feelings because the loved one left him by choice. Children need a safe place to talk about their feelings of loss and confusion. Even though a child may be young when a parent dies by suicide, he will deeply experience the loss himself and also witness the grief around him. The surviving parent and family members will be managing their own overwhelming feelings and may be much less available to meet the child's needs. A professional can help provide the words needed to explain to the child that his parent was very sick, has died, and will not be returning. Individual and family counseling can be extremely helpful in assisting the family to navigate through the stages of grief. The child may feel that he wants to be with the deceased parent and may want to mimic the parent's behaviors. At times like this, professional intervention is imperative. The death of a parent can be traumatic regardless of age or how the parent dies. The death of a parent by suicide is multilayered and may require professional intervention. As the layers peel back, with help and support, deep grief can be navigated and healing can occur over time.

Following a suicide, biological family members may experience concerns about their own predisposition to suicide. They can fear that because they share the same heredity with the deceased, they may at some point develop depression and suicidal tendencies. This concern can emerge strongly at times of stress and may become an intrusive worry about the self or about others in the family who may experience depression.

Those other than family members can also experience feelings of rejection in the aftermath of a completed suicide. Friends and close work mates may wonder why they were not important enough to the deceased to have been informed of their friend's despair before the suicide occurred. They may wonder whether their friendship was as meaningful to the person who died as it was to them. These feelings of being left without any word may create confusion and self-doubt about the importance of the relationship, and feelings of rejection can develop. As with other survivors, these feelings of rejection may be felt simultaneously with emotions of loss, guilt, anger, and profound sadness.

Gerrit Van Der Wal described bereavement following suicide as being different from other grief in several ways. He states that those bereaved by suicide may experience a heightened fear of being susceptible to suicide because of heredity, may embark on a prolonged search for motives, may more often deny the cause of death, and may experience a spiritual crisis and concerns about the afterlife.

Spiritual and religious questions may arise in a complex manner for the survivor of suicide. When someone passes from this life in what we consider to be a premature death, there are always questions about God and the afterlife. Where does the spirit go? Is a curtain drawn, and is that the end? Do our souls continue in another realm? Are our deceased loved ones watching over us from a happier place? Depending on our belief system and formal religion, the answers to each of these questions may differ. There may be anger at God and disbelief that a loving God could end a life before its natural time. Even when death occurs from natural old age, questions can remain about the afterlife and even the plan that God has for humankind. The partner of an elderly person may wonder why he has to be left behind and feel anger that God did not take him first. Core beliefs about life and the universe can be shaken, and a spiritual crisis may be a component of the grieving process.

Spiritual questions following a suicide are compounded by the fact that the deceased has taken her own life. Will there be a punishment in the afterlife because suicide is considered by some to be a sin? How can the survivor forgive his loved one for leaving him here alone? Anger, forgiveness, guilt, and fear all intertwine, and beliefs about God may be questioned. If a loving God can let this happen, then can the survivor continue to believe in this God? As these feelings and questions arise, it is important to embrace them and let them run their course, as with every other feeling and response to the death of the loved one. To block out or move around these feelings and questions is to avoid them, and they most likely will return in the future. The best way to manage the grief is to go through it with supports, not around it. It is most effective for healing to let the questions and the feelings emerge as they will naturally and to accept them as a part of a truly traumatic life event. As spirituality is questioned, the survivor may find it helpful to speak with someone in his church, synagogue, or other religious group. This reaching out will serve a multitude of purposes; an arena will be created for the spiritual questions to be asked, a support group will be developed, and the survivor can be connected with others who may have had the same experience. The survivor will be amazed at how many other survivors he finds when he has the courage to share his story. In some cases, after the deepest grief and anger is processed, the survivor will experience a new and clearer meaning in his life with his God and with the planet. Some survivors may not have had a previous connection or affiliation with a formal religious church or group. While there can be some initial anger at the universe, the loss of a loved one to suicide may create a new desire to reach out for spiritual connection and understanding. The attempt to make meaning after a suicide often involves one's spirituality, and this can take many forms. Meaning making can involve formal religion and traditional religious practices; it can involve informal practices of deepening intimate relationships and learning the importance of each day and every minute of living with loved ones. Clarity regarding just how finite life is may become crystallized after a traumatic death. The survivor can come to realize that he needs to seize each present moment with the living, because the next moment may bring a sudden change that can take away further opportunities to express what needs to be said.

Another aspect of spirituality following the death of a family member or friend can include finding forgiveness for the deceased and for oneself. When someone feels left and abandoned by a cherished other in a wide world full of complication, the process to forgiveness must, indeed, be a spiritual road. Equally spiritual is the road to forgiving oneself. Those last encounters with the deceased may not have been the best or the kindest, and the survivor may replay them again and again, wishing he had acted differently. Forgiving oneself is an important piece of healing; it can come with time and support.

Cultural responses to death and suicide may differ from country to country and ethnic group to ethnic group. Some stages of grief are universal, however, and the grieving of the suicide survivor can have many layers, regardless of the ethnic background of the survivor.

■ Coping Strategies

Specific coping strategies for complicated grief can assist the suicide survivor in managing reactions that can be overwhelming. The feelings that emerge after a suicide may initially be so strong that even remembering to breathe in a natural manner can be a chore. The survivor must remember that she has experienced a deep personal tragedy and that whatever she feels is a normal reaction to an abnormal event. Each survivor may have different set of responses to the suicide. Although many survivor reactions will be universal, there is no consistent road map for this journey. While one survivor may initially feel numbness and shock, another may feel rage or deep despair. Coping strategies can be used at any stage of grief and can modulate the extreme nature of response; the strategies described in this chapter can be adapted to fit the individual's unique path and place in her recovery.

It can be challenging to learn new coping skills at the time of a tragedy. It is, of course, best to have these skills in place before a traumatic event occurs—ah, but were all human beings so wise? Unfortunately, it is human nature to move through life with the hope that we will be one of the lucky ones who will be sheltered from devastating experiences. The assumption that any individual will not be faced with some major life event that is earth shattering is unlikely; yet preparation for dealing with adversity generally does not occur until unimaginable pain descends. Luckily, although it may be more difficult to learn coping skills in the midst of a traumatic experience, it is certainly possible. In fact, even if we do not often prepare for calamity, these skills are developed continually when personal disaster strikes.

Coping skills can be developed and utilized at any time following a suicide to create a buffer against both internal and external stressors. As the survivor learns these skills, he will be attempting to manage his own internal set of reactions, as well as dealing with external pressures from others around him. Internal and external stressors can be equally overwhelming and, combined, they can magnify to create a vortex of confusion, distress, and further despair for the survivor. The following pages will outline specific strategies for the survivor to deal with his complex internal reactions. Additionally, strategies for managing external pressures will be described for the survivor to adapt to his personal circumstances.

Internal Coping Skills

The first and most important coping skill for anyone following a traumatic event is to remember to breathe. This may sound ridiculous; however, when breathing is not regulated, emotions and physiology will automatically be out of sync. Irregular breathing patterns can generate a heightened emotional state and lead to anxiety and panic attacks. If the intake of breath is shallow and fast, the brain will not receive oxygen in an even fashion, and lightheadedness can occur. This emotional and physical deregulation caused by insufficient oxygen intake can create further disorientation, which will compound the many layers of stress that the survivor may experience. Reminding oneself to breathe steadily and deeply can have a positive effect in many ways. Deep breathing slows the heart rate, which, in turn, steadies blood flow and stabilizes physiology. Anxiety and subsequent panic that can sometimes be caused by lightheadedness due to shallow breathing can be circumvented when deep breathes are taken.

Focusing on breathing takes concentration, which can slow racing thoughts as one reminds oneself to breathe. This focus on breathing serves to momentarily take the survivor's mind off the tragedy, providing at least a few seconds of relief from conscious thought of the loss. Remembering to breathe slowly and deeply can inflate the lungs with oxygen, which then travels through the bloodstream to the brain. The brain, under stress from the event, is replenished with oxygen, and the trauma can be cognitively managed more effectively. Focusing on breathing is an effective relaxation technique that can be used at any stage in the grief reaction. The more that deep, slow breathing is used and practiced, the better the survivor will feel. Learning to breathe slowly must be a conscious process, and it is an easy skill that one can learn at any time. Although the skill is a simple one, its positive effects should not be underestimated.

Gathering support is another important internal coping skill. It is truly a skill to be able to choose the people who can be most available for comfort following a tragic loss. Some of the usual supports may not be the best choice following a suicide. These individuals could be experiencing their own grief, they may have their own issues with the loss, or they may have a morbid case of curiosity about the circumstances of the suicide. It is important for the survivor to be discerning about who he seeks for solace. It may take several attempts to find the best supports; the survivor needs to keep trying until there is someone who can listen without judgment. In fact, if it is possible, it can be most effective to build a support network so that more than one person is available as a confidant. Although the survivor may want to be isolated and alone with his grief, it often helps to allow others to share the grief. While the support person(s) may not be able to completely comprehend what the survivor is experiencing, a good listener can be a wonderful outlet. Building a network of important others requires some skill in determining who will be a good listener and not impose her own thoughts, questions, and beliefs on the survivor. There may be some false starts as the survivor begins to share his story; it is important for the survivor to set boundaries or withdraw from someone who is not supportive. It is equally important for the survivor to trust his instincts and to surround himself with others who provide comfort, support, and understanding.

The survivor is vulnerable, and the task of finding good supports may feel daunting. There may be some fear on the part of the survivor that, because of the stigma of suicide, she will be judged by others. Reaching out to an objective counselor can be a wonderful way to obtain support when there is fear of stigma or important others do not really seem to understand. The professional is trained to listen and be a guide through the stages of grief. Contacting a therapist can be a powerful step in building supports. The therapist will be able to assist the survivor in building and practicing some of the coping skills discussed in this chapter. Many therapists specialize in grieving and loss; during the initial call to a counselor, the survivor can ask whether the counselor has experience in working with survivors of suicide. If not, the counselor should be able to refer the survivor to another therapist who has this experience. It is not always a necessary step to obtain professional help, but it can be useful if other supports are not available, or in addition to the survivor's personal supports.

Support groups can also be especially helpful to some survivors. These groups may include an informal network composed of others who have experienced a death by suicide. In a group, family members and friends can share their stories of personal loss, grief, and coping. These groups can be located through the local mental health hotline, the local mental health clinic, or the American Foundation for Suicide Prevention (AFSP) at 1-888-333-AFSP or online at www.afsp.org. The AFSP also has a Survivor e-Network that can be accessed through their Web site. Other support groups may be facilitated by a professional, and these groups can be located through the local mental health clinic or information hotline. Generally, professionally led groups are more formal in structure, and these grief groups may include members who have experienced several types of loss, not only a death to suicide. For many survivors, sharing their grief with other survivors can be a powerful healing tool and one more way to cope with a catastrophic loss.

Expressing feelings is another internal coping mechanism that is important for the survivor. All feelings are acceptable and normal following such an extreme loss, and these feelings may fluctuate rapidly. One moment the survivor may feel sadness, and in the next minute or hour anger or guilt may emerge. Each individual mourns in her own way and at her own pace; the survivor needs to be gentle with herself and let the process happen in its own time. The survivor may not be used to or comfortable with the emergence of extreme feelings that grief can bring, but the expression of these emotions helps to move the individual closer to acceptance.

It is entirely up to the survivor to decide whether he wants to share his feelings and reveal the fact that he has had a loved one die by suicide. It can be extraordinarily helpful to have a few trusted people available to feel safe enough with to disclose the nature of the event and subsequent feelings. Some survivors may be private people and, in general, may not share their emotions or life story with others. Other survivors may feel shame or guilt about the suicide and not want to talk about it. Every individual has the right to decide what information he wants to disclose or withhold. Sharing emotions with those who may not be appropriately responsive could be potentially harmful and increase the pain of the survivor, so it is important to choose supports carefully. When choosing supports, whether formal or informal, it is helpful to find people who will cherish and honor the survivor's feelings as they emerge.

Expressing feelings is a part of the coping package of recovery. Along with the expression of feelings comes the telling of one's story about the suicide. Many of the same principles apply to telling the story as they do to the expression of feelings. The survivor may choose not to share anything about the death, she may choose to make full disclosure, or she may have several versions of information that she provides to different people, depending on the circumstances. For example, the survivor may have a few good supports with whom she shares all of the details and resulting emotions from the suicide. These chosen recipients, one hopes, will be the people who the survivor knows will listen to her without judgment and comfort her without imposing their own agenda. For others in the support network, the survivor may have a brief version of her story to tell, and for others yet the survivor has the choice not to disclose any information at all. It can be challenging to set boundaries when curious people ask deliberate and intrusive questions about a suicide. The survivor should establish a handful of "sound bytes" or short responses that can be as simple as "I am not comfortable talking about this" or "The details of the death are too hard for me to discuss." It can be helpful for the survivor to develop comfortable language to use when approached by someone who has questions that the survivor does not want to answer. This protective language is an internal coping skill that can be developed and used to set boundaries with external negative forces. When the feelings and images of the suicide are raw and painful, the survivor may experience a need to withdraw and wall herself off from the world. This is another normal response to an abnormal event. In general, the emotions following the suicide of a loved one may be extreme because of the finality and violent nature of the death. Professional intervention is imperative only if the survivor experiences suicidal thought herself or if a survivor's feelings or responses profoundly affect her functioning for an extended period of time. Suicidal thoughts and extreme, prolonged emotion that affects daily functioning are not normal grief and should be assessed by a professional.

The survivor may not feel the energy to implement major coping mechanisms; these skills may seem daunting to develop and beyond the capacity of the survivor as he struggles through the first days and weeks following the suicide of a loved one. Other simple skills are available that the survivor may not think of as coping strategies, but that serve to soothe a battered soul. Each tiny effort that the survivor can

Lafourche Parish Library
Thibodaux, Louisiana

take to nurture himself may require a Herculean effort, but these efforts can add up and generate a path toward healing. The survivor can utilize small daily internal coping techniques that can be cumulative in the journey back from despair. It is important for the survivor to think and act in small increments, particularly if they cannot tolerate anything harder. Small steps lead to larger steps; it may be a slow journey, but there can always be progress.

The survivor can begin her recovery in many small ways. Taking a few moments each day and standing in the sun can serve as a short rejuvenation. As the survivor feels the warmth penetrate her skin, this exercise begins to form a sensation that the earth is trying to give back some of what it has taken away. The vitamin D from the sun provides a physical benefit to compound the momentary emotional pleasure of the warmth. This exercise of standing in the sun provides the survivor with fresh air—the impulse may be to isolate and withdraw, and taking a few minutes each day to step outside breaks the cycle of isolation. It may be helpful for the survivor to purchase a small living thing and watch it grow. A plant that sits on a window sill or seeds that the survivor can plant and witness their sprouting may provide hope. A plant requires little care and can give back important reminders of the life cycle.

The survivor should maintain a routine schedule. Keeping a balance during the grief cycle can be challenging, and the comfort of what is usual and expected can help the survivor maintain equilibrium. Going to bed at the usual time, trying not to sleep away the day, and eating at the same time as always will help to keep the survivor's body rhythm natural. The survivor may have little appetite during the initial stages of grief, and the last thing he may feel like doing may be eating. Making sure that at least small meals are taken at the usual time and sleep patterns are kept will assist the survivor in maintaining his physical health. These usual patterns also provide a manner through which to fortify internal structure when everything else can seem to be falling apart.

It may be tempting for the survivor to increase alcohol or drug use if that is a way she has coped with emotional issues in the past. The use of drugs and alcohol may, at first, seem to be soothing for the survivor; however, most substances are also depressants that can complicate an already compromised emotional and physical reaction. Additionally, many of these substances can create tolerance and subsequent addiction if used over time. Prescribed medications may be helpful for use during certain stages of the grieving process. Individuals who experience extreme anxiety, sleep disruption, or ongoing symptoms of depression might benefit from either the short-term use of prescribed antianxiety medications, sleep aids, or a longer-term course of antidepressants. If

the need for medication arises, it should be prescribed by someone in the medical profession who can monitor the effects of the drug.

Other small rituals, such as pouring a cup of special, soothing tea or taking a warm bath or shower, can help to slowly soothe a broken heart. These rituals may require a trip to a local health food store or boutique to purchase just the right tea or bath salts. This journey will help the survivor to step outside her pain for a period of time and join the world. As the survivor embarks on a concrete task of self-care, she begins to fill up the internal hole that has been created from the loss.

As the healing process progresses, other rituals can be helpful for the survivor that are more specific to dealing with the loss of her loved one. It may be wise to let some time pass from the first torrent of grief to implement these rituals; however, there is not a right or wrong way to utilize rituals. Some survivors may need to find a way to express themselves immediately through the use of rituals, whereas others may need to wait until the heightened aftershocks have passed. Rituals that are specific to the loss of a family member or friend can include writing a letter to the deceased, building a small memorial that includes the loved one's effects, or creating a memory scrapbook filled with items, pictures, and thoughts about the deceased. Rituals can be designed by the survivor alone or with important others for support or to share thoughts and memories.

Another way in which survivors can care for themselves is to prepare for future events or circumstances that may trigger memories of the loved one. Birthdays (both the deceased's and the survivor's), anniversaries, holidays, the date of the suicide, and other memorable days can renew a torrent of memories and feelings. Identifying and planning for the upcoming dates that may trigger emotional upheaval can be useful. For some survivors, having a ritual to acknowledge the deceased on certain days may be helpful; for other survivors, staying active and having supports around them can be most beneficial. Remembering some of the coping skills discussed earlier in this chapter and using them during these times can ease some of the pain. The goal of recovery is not to forget the deceased; it is to be able to remember with less hurt. Time will help with this goal; in the meantime, the skills noted in this chapter can assist the survivor in blunting some of the deepest angst.

Managing External Pressures

During this devastating time, when an individual's emotional resources are the most strained, the survivor must develop and implement coping skills to manage his internal process of grieving. In addition to managing his own internal world, the survivor must navigate the world around him. Unfortunately, the survivor cannot necessarily count on others to understand him and to act in a manner that is most beneficial to him. The survivor must be aware of his surroundings. If the survivor finds he is being harmed by the "helpful other," he needs to set boundaries to protect himself.

One of the first experiences that the survivor may have is with the local police department. This department may be in a metropolitan area or in a small community. The location is not necessarily relevant to how law enforcement will react; the survivor can find either kindness or a lack of humanity in either place. The police officer who knows how to be gentle and careful with questions, or to offer a cup of coffee or a tissue, can make a great difference in a survivor's world. At times like these, small kindnesses can mean a tremendous amount to the survivor. The officers who have the qualities that show humanity may not have learned these traits through training; they generally come from the heart. Unfortunately, some law enforcement officials do not understand that a survivor needs gentle care. Some officers may present with their own history of trauma and stress from their current work load. These officers may have their own triggers that have been activated by the suicide and may move through the legal process at a pace that does not match the survivor's needs. Many survivors are in shock at the stage in which law enforcement is involved and have a difficult time even being emotionally present for questions. Some survivors have their own history with the police and may feel intimidated and fearful that they will be blamed for the suicide. The survivor should feel equipped to set boundaries with law enforcement when needed; this can be challenging during a law enforcement process that needs to move quickly through evidence when it is fresh. A suicide can be considered a crime scene, and even this knowledge may affect the survivor. If the survivor cannot initially set boundaries with law enforcement, it is best to find an advocate in the legal system to help her to navigate her rights and the law. Legal counsel can provide clarity for the survivor about her rights; it can also provide further legal answers to questions that may arise regarding the completed suicide. The police may place a hold on the body of the deceased until it is determined whether a physical autopsy is required by law. This can be necessary to determine the exact cause of death. The surviving family member may either be in favor of the autopsy or have other wishes for the deceased. Legal counsel can be instrumental to the survivor in understanding her rights. If a survivor is questioned by law enforcement and does not feel equipped to answer questions, she has the right to ask for an attorney to be present before further proceedings.

Other outside influences can feel overwhelming to the survivor such as inquisitive others. These people may want to help, but their questions can feel intrusive. Some survivors may not be ready to answer questions or to talk about their deceased loved one, especially just following news of the suicide. They may be experiencing shock or disbelief. Repeated questions from concerned others can create further trauma for the survivor. Setting boundaries with intrusive others is important. As stated earlier, setting boundaries can require the use of internal coping skills and emotional energy from the survivor, who is already feeling emotionally depleted. Using simple sound bytes such as "I can't talk about this now" or "I really need to take some time for myself before I am ready to talk about this" can be useful in setting boundaries. As discussed, it may be helpful to establish one or two simple statements to use repeatedly when others ask questions. Survivors may feel like others are watching them; they may feel vulnerable, and it is good to recognize this because they are, indeed, vulnerable. They have just experienced an unimaginable tragedy, and others may not understand the depth of the loss or just may be curious about how the survivor will respond. If the survivor has a trusted friend that he can use as an "ambassador" to provide concerned others with information about his progress, this can serve to stem the flow of direct phone calls and questions. This ambassador or designated person can become the link between the survivor and the outside world until the survivor has the emotional energy to deal with it himself. In this way, boundaries can be set by another who will manage the external pressures for the survivor.

The survivor needs to take her own time and focus on her own needs in her unique healing process. Some survivors need to talk; others need to withdraw a bit and focus inward. Each survivor is different, and there is no right or wrong way to heal. If a survivor feels overwhelmed by external pressures, however, her own healing will be affected.

Saying no can be challenging even under the best of circumstances. How does the survivor say no to someone kind who wants to bring him a home-cooked dinner and sit with him while he cries? How does the survivor ignore the telephone the fourth time a colleague has called from work wondering how he is doing? These circumstances are some of the external challenges that the survivor may face. The last thing that the survivor wants to do may be to eat a meal or have someone watch him cry. Compound these single examples with the probability that several people have offered to make food or come by for a visit. The telephone answering machine probably has several messages from people wanting to help. The survivor needs to recognize that it is okay to say no, and this is especially important when feeling overwhelmed. If the survivor can designate one or two trusted friends to respond to calls from others who want to help, the pressure to talk to everyone will be relieved. These ambassadors can report any information to the concerned others that the survivor wants them to know. This will ease the responsibility and burden of the survivor tremendously.

When the survivor is a parent who has children who are also experiencing grief, special circumstances require specific attention. The parent may be emotionally unavailable to her children because of the level of her own grief. Depending on the developmental stage and environment that they are in, children may experience and demonstrate the loss differently. Some children may not understand the disappearance of their loved one, and the subsequent pain and unavailability of the remaining parent. They may be fearful, withdraw, act out, or show their feelings in any variety of ways. Professional help is often a good intervention for the child who has lost a parent to any sudden death. The professional can help the surviving parent talk to the child about the nature of the death, as appropriate. The counselor can guide the child through some of what he may be feeling. Children sometimes have magical thinking and may believe that their parent or other loved one will be returning. They may hope that they can leave and be with the deceased parent, or they may somehow believe that they are responsible for their parent's death. The surviving parent is experiencing her own pain and may not clearly be able to see that her child is experiencing deep hurt. Professional counseling can be a supportive intervention for the family. The counselor will not only help the child navigate these difficult waters, but also will provide the parent with additional skills to assist the child and to cope herself.

The survivor may have siblings or parents who can be experiencing emotional turmoil from the death of a loved one by suicide at the same time. Sharing grief can be helpful at times, but the survivor may feel as if he is comforting everyone else around him. Making space for one's own process is crucial. For example, if one parent has completed suicide and left another parent behind, an adult child may feel an obligation to put the grief of his living parent before his own. Each survivor has equally traumatic loss; each survivor has his own path in recovery. Supporting the other survivor may be needed to some extent; however, it is critical to focus on one's own needs and journey. Family therapy can be helpful to some families, while individual counseling can be beneficial to others. Many communities have centers for grieving persons, and these can be located through the local community information hotline or mental health center.

▨ Making New Meaning

Ivan Smith states that survivors proceed through three levels of making meaning following a loved one's suicide. The first level is described as the making of temporary meaning, which is seized by the survivor in the initial stages of grief without much thought due to shock and numbness. This meaning is described as shifting over time as the reality of the suicide sets in. The second level of meaning noted by Smith is called transitional meaning, and this type of meaning is one in which the survivor tries to make sense of the chaos that the suicide has created in her life. These applied meanings can help the survivor to navigate through the funeral and the first months, and sometimes years, following the death. The final level of meaning making described by Smith is called transformational meaning. This is the kind of meaning that shifts belief in a profound way. For some, the transformational meaning may never come; for others, it may take years. For most, the initial stages of grief must be navigated before the survivor can move to this deeper place of understanding. How could this suicide have a purpose? How could this suicide have been a positive event for the deceased? How could this death be a gift of help to someone else? Transformational meaning helps the survivor to find answers to some of these difficult questions. Many of the survivors who experience transformational meaning have gone on to establish recovery programs for other survivors of suicide. They have taken their loss and worked to find a way to reach others to change their lives, and in doing so, their own lives are changed. Smith describes transformational meaning as continually shifting. Meaning making is a process that regenerates and renews. In combination with other sources of meaning, newer cocreations of thought and behavior can emerge, ever moving in fresh directions. Following a tremendous loss such as the death of a loved one to suicide, this transformational meaning can take time. Feelings and behaviors are a journey; each path is different.

▪ Case Example Revisited: The Survivor Transformed

Richard had thoughts about dying following the suicide of his mentor. He struggled with physical and emotional pain, including guilt, loss, thoughts of suicide himself, shock, cold, and stomach pain. He felt immobile for several months. He went through many of the stages of loss and did reach out for help. He felt his despair; he acted out his anger by throwing things out his window. The traditional route of counseling was not helpful to him, so he tried a less traditional guided exercise of rebirthing, which left him feeling even more vulnerable. Richard sought meaning even in the early stages of his grief, even though he had had some premonition that his mentor would kill himself.

The most helpful interventions for Richard included using his support systems and talking to others about his grief. He had a great need to tell his story and to be heard. For Richard, his wife and friends served as the best listeners. Richard's dreams also greatly helped and comforted to him. The first dream that he had following the death of his mentor was a turning point for Richard.

Today, Richard wants to tell his story to anyone he can help to recover from the death of a loved one. This is transformational grief. Richard has chosen not to forget his mentor, but rather to use their relationship and his death to help others through their own pain.

Other survivors will have different stories and ways that they will come to make meaning of their loss. Richard's story is only one story of 300,000 survivors. Each survivor has his own unique and human way to deal with what may first appear to be a meaningless act.

6 ■ ■ ■

Surviving a Patient Suicide

■ Case Example: Frozen in Time

She stared out the windows at the trees, without seeing anything at all. She knew that unless she could pull herself together, she would not be in any condition to see her next patient. She could not remember a time that she had felt so disconnected from everything. She simply wanted to sit still and stare at the snow-covered limbs while the world went on revolving around her.

When she divorced her husband five years earlier, she had experienced a searing pain that came and went, but she had still been able to function. During that period in her life, she had found that she could put her emotions on hold during an hour-long therapy session. Then, in the 10 minutes she scheduled between patients, she would double over with the emerging feelings. She had amazed herself when, miraculously, she could pull herself together for her next appointment. In fact, looking back, it seemed that her work had somehow created an organizing force in her life that had helped her to survive.

Today, there was no organization to bind the thoughts and emotions. She flipped through her appointment book aimlessly and realized that she needed to cancel her day but did not have the energy to look up her patients' numbers and make the calls. Besides, what would she say? "I'm sorry, one of my other patients killed herself last month, and I don't feel competent to see you?" Or, "I've decided that I'm not really very good at being a therapist, so I want to refer you to another psychologist?" Or even, "I'm afraid you made a mistake when you put your trust in me for help; I really don't know what I am doing?"

The appointment book again found itself open to the page last month that she now knew by heart, patient to patient. Sandwiched in the middle of the afternoon was the young man's name, and her eyes glued to her handwriting as if staring at the page long enough would make him come back to life.

She had begun to treat him two years ago for clinical depression. She was a seasoned psychologist and easily diagnosed his difficulties and put a treatment plan in place. The young man responded well to medication and cognitive therapy, and had begun to put his life back in order. Then, a month ago he had come to his session in crisis after learning he had lost his job. As they knew each other well, she had assessed him in a straight-forward fashion and designed a safety plan with him in the event he would experience suicidal feelings. He had denied having suicidal thoughts during her assessment and had agreed to the safety plan. Because they had a long-standing relationship, she had believed he would follow the plan and call her for help if he felt suicidal. At the session's close, he had seemed reluctant to leave. She had been aware of her next patient in the waiting room and had set up a follow-up appointment with him, encouraging him to call her if he needed to talk between sessions.

She could clearly remember where she had been when the call had come, almost as one of the clearest moments of her life. Everything around her had seemed to crystallize in place. The voice at the end of the receiver had told her that her patient had hung himself. They had found her appointment card in his wallet. It had happened on the same evening of his last visit with her.

She felt that she should know what to do, how to deal with the inertia and paralysis that she was experiencing. Instead, every movement was robotic; each word spoken felt like it echoed in an empty room. She certainly had experienced the stress of her work at other times in her career. She had worked with children who were abused, with adults who lived through unimaginable horrors, and with people who were in the last stage of terminal illness. Although she had agonized with the losses of these patients, none of these had prepared her for what she was now experiencing.

She could not talk about what had happened in any detail with her new husband because of the ethics of confidentiality. He was supportive with the limited information she had provided him and could understand her distress in a peripheral kind of way.

Her colleagues only spoke of such professional tragedies in what seemed to her to be a superficial manner; she did not believe the depth of her angst would be understood if she went to them. She felt as if she were alone on a beach on which the sand was shifting and she could not gain her footing. Others walked by her firm-footed a few yards away on sand that had been hardened by the ocean and did not notice her struggle or reach out a hand to help. Part of her understood that her colleagues did not lack empathy. Instinctively, she knew that their avoidance came from their own vulnerabilities and not knowing what to do or say.

▦ The Professional

The most poignant moments in a person's life often occur when there is what appears to be a tragic event. This event may be personal or professional and can be so momentous that, after it occurs, nothing seems to be the same. A shattering of the core self takes place, and for a time, it can appear that we do not know ourselves or those closest to us. The once-familiar roads we drive look different; our office seems as if it must belong to someone else. Simple acts we have always taken for granted, such as dressing in the morning or sipping a cup of coffee, become movements that feel foreign, frivolous, or meaningless. Moving through the day takes tremendous energy. It is as if we are in a new country in which no one speaks our language. The things that we were once sure that we knew are no longer, and we feel like a stranger alone in the universe. How can this be? How could any single event shake us so to the core of our beings? And when it does, how do we recover? How do we take the tragedy and use it to examine ourselves and grow from it?

When a tragedy such as a patient suicide occurs in a professional's life, nothing seems the same. In the shadow of a patient suicide, the caregiver is left to manage the aftermath, both personally and professionally. The tragedy of the loss of a patient in such a violent way can be completely disorganizing. A patient's suicide is the clinician's worst fear, and when it occurs, time can stand still. The usual routine of patient care is questioned; each sentence uttered by the provider suddenly becomes a matter of life or death. Progress notes that are written become a chronicle of care that either demonstrates the talent of the provider or the way in which the caregiver missed some signal that could have saved a patient's life. Other patients' words become sinister, and each sentence is reviewed for suicidal intent. Self-doubt regarding clinical judgment and beliefs and fantasies of silent accusations and criticisms by colleagues and supervisors may affect the treatment of others on the provider's caseload.[1]

In medical and clinical training programs, providers have not been taught how to manage the overwhelming and complicated responses experienced when a patient is lost to suicide. According to the AFSP, every 18 minutes someone in the United States dies by suicide and someone is left behind to try to make sense of it.[2] In many of these instances, one of the survivors of suicide may be the clinician who has treated the individual. Although supports are in place for family members and friends of people who have died by suicide, the caregiver has had little formal process for her own recovery. Herbert Hendin and others stated, "National studies conducted in the 1980s indicate that one-half of psychiatrists and one-quarter of psychologists had experienced the suicide of a patient."[3] These statistics do not include other types of clinicians or nonrespondents to the study and, in fact, this number is probably much higher.

The general clinical practitioner greets each day with a full schedule of patients to treat. These patients come with a wide array of issues that may have mild to significant impact on their daily functioning. The clinician enters into a contract, either verbal or nonverbal, with the patient to address the presenting problem. The clinician and the patient then embark together on a journey unlike any other. It is a journey based on trust, relationship, courage, and even faith. It is a relationship that has an impact not only on the patient but also on the clinician. The successes of the journey are celebrated by both partners, setbacks are examined, and new trails are blazed. The patient shares deep recesses of himself in a new way with the clinician who is his compatriot. Even in one short appointment, constructs between the patient and the clinician can be developed, and as time goes on, the meaning that each of the dyad finds is fortified and deepens. Although the journey belongs to the patient, it is shared and magnified by the clinician. Each patient has a unique and sacred relationship with the professional; each hour is marked by difference from that before or after it. The practitioner is not a bystander in this relationship. The provider becomes embedded in the patient's world and, by the nature of the unique therapeutic interactions, has influence and interest in the patient's life story.

Irving Steingart describes a model that offers a way to understand the love that develops between clinician and patient, a love that is not based on transference, but on a love of truth and on an understanding of the patient's psychic reality. Steingart postulates that the love between patient and caregiver is mutual and develops in the clinician as a response to the patient's presentation. The provider is not a blank screen, immune to reciprocal affection. The provider is a part of the relationship that, in the best of circumstances, leads the patient to create corrective change.[4]

The value of the therapeutic relationship cannot be minimized. The wealth of literature and research on the therapeutic alliance demonstrates just how crucial the relationship is to positive patient outcome. According to Richard Summers and Jacques Barber, "The therapeutic alliance stands out to be a measurable phenomenon that has been shown to have a robust effect on treatment outcome.[5]

In light of the fact that the caregiving relationship is of such importance, it is curious that the caregiver seldom has been considered in the literature when a patient dies by suicide. This is especially puzzling considering that "at least one in five mental health professionals lose(s) a patient to suicide," according to Tori DeAngelis.[6] Emergency room physicians are left to their own devices when a patient is admitted for a suicide attempt. Larry Zaroff said, "I quickly consult the *Merck Manual* but find no reference to suicide and multiple injuries. We are on our own."[7]

What appears to be ambivalence in the clinical community is primarily played out with silence when a colleague has experienced a patient death by suicide. The clinician who has experienced the loss is immersed in his own world of professional and personal pain, and surrounding colleagues bow their heads and continue in their own routines as if grateful to have "dodged the bullet" in their own practice. Unfortunately, even caregivers who experience a client death and attempt to talk about the loss may still feel dismissed as the professional community glosses over the magnitude of the event.

Carl Jung wrote at length regarding the collective unconscious and the power of the unrecognized pattern by families and communities, such as the medical and mental health community. He described these collective representations as spontaneous, involuntary manifestations and not intentional occurrences. Jung further stated that this collective unconscious is the part of the psyche that retains and transmits the common inheritance of humankind.[8] The medical and mental health communities have their own way of being unconscious to the suffering of the provider at the time of a patient death by suicide. Kay Jamison and R. J. Baldessarini stated,

In the literature on suicide, among the least commonly discussed topics is the reaction of mental health professionals when one of their patients in treatment commits suicide. This relative silence is especially noteworthy given that a substantial proportion of the more than 30,000 individuals who commit suicide yearly in the United States have been in treatment with a mental health professional.[9]

The inability of both the medical and mental health communities to care for themselves or one of their own in a time of greatest professional and personal crisis is a curious phenomenon. In the medical world, the physician has not been taught to process the death and dying of his patients, and certainly not to grieve. Resident psychiatrists are rarely coached on methods to manage a patient's suicide. Mental health clinicians are trained to be aware of the affective world around them and to be vigilant to their internal reactions to the presentation of others. In the mental health profession, however, there also remains ambivalence, avoidance, and antipathy when the worst-feared scenario of a patient death occurs. Why do providers retreat to unconscious movement away from their own reactions and the reactions of their colleagues who have experienced such a loss firsthand? The phenomenon of provider minimization when a patient dies by suicide is dangerous, because the treating caregiver many subsequently carry both a conscious and unconscious wish to avoid the treatment of other patients who present with depressive or suicidal tendencies.

A patient suicide can occur at any time during a professional's career, and when it happens, it can be a life-altering event. Eric Plankun stated, "A patient's suicide is an occupational hazard that leaves a torrent of personal and professional aftershocks. It makes us wonder why we didn't go into ophthalmology."[10] Providers may experience a multitude of symptoms in reaction to a patient suicide. For the younger caregiver, such as an intern, it may be the pivotal event that leads her to question or even change her career. Older, more seasoned providers who have managed to treat hundreds of patients over the years without tragedy may suddenly find themselves questioning their ability to diagnose and treat. The thought that a patient may successfully complete suicide remains one of the greatest fears of any provider, and once the practitioner has a patient who completes suicide, this fear can heighten. Feelings of self-doubt can lead the provider to become hypervigilant with other patients who are not suicidal. Instead of being able to provide objective treatment, the provider's abilities may become clouded by fears of another potential loss to suicide. This hypervigilance may result in treatment procedures that are not warranted and hospitalizations that are not necessary. The caregiver may experience intrusive thoughts about the suicide that affect his daily functioning. These thoughts may occur throughout the course of the day and create a distraction to the work at hand, thereby affecting the professional's effective functioning. Concentration can be affected as the thoughts intrude; other medical and mental health issues presented by the patient can be completely missed. Sleep can be disrupted as the intrusive thoughts swirl at night and the practitioner replays the treatment leading up to the suicide again and again, wondering whether he could have done anything to avert the tragedy. Missed sleep may add to difficulties concentrating during the day, and the provider's functioning is further compromised. At work, as the provider's skills diminish, problems may escalate with the supervisor, who may not be aware of the inner turmoil the provider is experiencing. A negative vortex begins and can spin out of control.

Each survivor of patient suicide may have a unique way of responding to the event. Some may attempt to block out thoughts of the suicide and move forward without acknowledging loss, perhaps acting out their reactions unconsciously. Others may experience some of the self-doubt, hypervigilance, intrusive thoughts, and sleep disturbance that have been noted. Yet others may have nightmares and use substances to induce sleep and to self-medicate. This use of substances can be particularly destructive to the professional's career and personal life. The toll of a patient suicide can manifest itself in the professional in many ways and degrees, depending on the provider's own coping resources, resiliency, and supports. Some professionals may begin to avoid work, showing up late for appointments and calling in sick. There may be an adverse impact on the provider's personal relationships as the caregiver carries the wounds from the suicide from work to home.

A patient's suicide can have many implications for the functioning of the provider. Therefore, it would seem imperative that a mechanism be in place to assist the professional survivor of a patient suicide. One such mechanism, psychological autopsy, is detailed in the remainder of this chapter.

■ The Psychological Autopsy

The process of psychological autopsy has been utilized in the past in many ways to address the death of a patient by suicide. Most of these autopsies are designed to understand the state of mind of the person who has taken his own life. For example, one definition of the psychological autopsy is

> an attempt to clarify the nature of death by focusing on the psychological aspects of the death. Its primary purpose is to understand the circumstances and state of mind of the victim at the time of death. The procedure involves the reconstruction of the circumstances of the victim, together with details of behaviors and events leading to the time of death.[11]

This model of psychological autopsy is designed to assist those who may be investigating the suicide for legal reasons. It is not a process that is necessarily helpful to the treating provider.

In the early fifties, the traditional medical pathological conference was adapted to evaluate ambiguous deaths in the Los Angeles coroner's office.[12] Edwin Shneidman and his colleagues further developed and adapted the pathology conference as a model for health professionals following a patient suicide so they might "attempt to identify the motives, lifestyles and feelings of the patients by reviewing their own deservations, including private feelings toward the patient." Describing activities that reduce the aftereffects of a traumatic event with the term "postvention," Shneidman and others emphasized the importance of intervention after suicide.[13]

Considering the number of caregivers who are affected by a patient suicide, relatively limited research in the literature on psychological autopsy is geared primarily for the professional's recovery. This chapter addresses the specific use for psychological autopsy that is focused on the professional's healing from a patient suicide. This method of autopsy can provide the clinician the opportunity to review the case, process her feelings of loss and responsibility with trusted colleagues, and receive help with coping mechanisms. When this psychological autopsy works effectively, the provider is left with a sense of closure. Although some feelings regarding the suicide may always remain for the clinician, she will be less likely to interfere with personal and professional functioning.

Many clinician-survivors of suicide have personally experienced the layers of trauma that accompany a patient suicide. In the months and years following a patient's death by suicide, these caregivers have struggled to find a way to make sense of the tragedy both in their professional and personal lives and in their spiritual worlds. At the time of their patient's suicide, they feel alone and without resources for support. Although they may have many trusted colleagues, none seems to understand the depth of the despair that accompanies this kind of loss. Some providers, in their fumbling for help and attempt to make meaning of the suicide, may reach out to a current mentor or someone from another period in their lives. The mentor may be reminded of a loss she may have experienced at some time in her own career. As the mentor gently guides the provider through the course of treatment with the deceased patient and the feelings of responsibility, loss, and pain, she may share her own story of patient loss. The mentor may be suffering in some parallel way with the caregiver. In many ways, the losses are universal; each professional who loses a patient to suicide faces a multitude of feelings and responses. Many professionals, however, do not have the opportunity to process and heal from the trauma they experience when a patient takes his own life.

▓ Psychological Autopsy for the Professional

There are many definitions of psychological autopsy, as has been noted. The method of psychological autopsy that is outlined next is a relatively simple model designed to promote the healing process for the professional from the death of a patient by suicide. This method can be used by psychologists, therapists, counselors, caseworkers, psychiatrists, medical doctors, case managers, and anyone who has had a professional relationship with a client. The model designed is similar to that of a crisis debriefing model, and in this case, the psychological autopsy has three phases. In the first phase, the individual or group participants are guided through a cognitive process of what is remembered, or a case review. The second phase provides an opportunity for emotions regarding the event to be expressed. In the final phase, cognitive strategies and resources for the survivor are explored. This psychological autopsy is not an investigation, nor is it a legal review. The sole purpose of the autopsy is to provide a safe outlet for the surviving professional to talk about the loss of her patient and to have colleagues offer supportive coping strategies and resources.

The presentation in this chapter of this model for psychological autopsy for the professional can be altered to fit the circumstances and need. There is no "right or wrong"; best practice often involves simple compassion and professional instinct on the part of the facilitator. Members of the autopsy group will be professional peers and, therefore, will have some understanding of the work that the surviving professional has done with the deceased. Each member of the group will bring his or her own life history and events from which to offer support, advice, and coping skills.

The Facilitator

The psychological autopsy that is designed to assist the professional in her recovery from the death of a patient by suicide may be conducted by a trusted past supervisor, colleague, or mentor. The facilitator holds the single most important role in the psychological autopsy. This person should be knowledgeable about loss, recovery, coping skills, and group process. The facilitator must have the basic counseling skills necessary to guide the autopsy from the case review and the feelings that emerge toward helpful coping skills. Most professionals who work with potentially suicidal individuals are trained in these skills and, therefore, should be readily available to assist with an autopsy. The most important qualifications for the facilitator are that she possess gentle wisdom and compassion and that she can assist with the group process.

This facilitator for the autopsy may be chosen by the professional who has been affected by the suicide. If the surviving professional does not have a requested facilitator, then the supervisor or a colleague may recommend someone to take this role. The professional should agree to the choice of facilitator and feel comfortable with the leader who has been chosen. It is most helpful if the facilitator is objective and has not had any supervisory responsibility for the case that is going to be discussed. If the facilitator has had supervisory responsibility for the case in which there has been a recent suicide, he may be experiencing some of his own reactions to the suicide. He may not be objective enough to be helpful to the treating professional. The supervisor can mimic the treating professional and have his own autopsy, or the supervisor may decide to discuss the case in his own supervision, with a mentor or colleague. The ripple effects of a patient suicide can be profound and affect not only the treating professional, but also the supervisor, the system, and colleagues.

The direct supervisor should not facilitate or even join the autopsy for several reasons. As stated, if the supervisor has had direct exposure to the case, she could be experiencing her own direct reactions, which could interfere with the treating professional's experience. Additionally, the supervisor may be in an evaluative role with the professional. Even if it is explicitly stated that the autopsy would not be a part of any evaluative process, the treating professional may be fearful of judgment. If available, a trusted past supervisor would be an appropriate facilitator. A past supervisor may be someone who the surviving professional trusts and holds in esteem, and who knows the professional's work well. This type of facilitator's involvement could deepen the healing that can occur in a psychological autopsy as a result of having someone present with whom the professional can be vulnerable.

The Group

The psychological autopsy can include just the facilitator and the professional in a dyad; the facilitator, one other colleague, and the professional; or the facilitator, the professional, and a few trusted colleagues. This type of smaller group may feel comforting to the professional and help her to feel less vulnerable; conversely, a larger group may be too diluted and can create feelings of exposure. Others invited into the autopsy should have a professional identity similar to that of the treating caregiver and should be invited or accepted by the professional who has had the patient suicide. For example, if a doctor has experienced the patient suicide, it can be most helpful to have other doctors as participants. A homogeneous group is necessary so that the surviving professional feels that an atmosphere has been set for understanding, support, and nonjudgment. Group members may come from the professional's circle of colleagues. If the professional feels comfortable with those who are present, she is more likely to be able to talk about what she needs to begin her recovery process. This level of comfort is necessary so that the professional will feel safe enough to express her thoughts and feelings about the course of treatment and her relationship with the patient. The facilitator may ask the professional whom she would like to participate in the autopsy and should respect the survivor's request. The suggested participants in a psychological autopsy usually include the facilitator, the surviving professional, and two colleagues; however, an autopsy can be equally effective if the professional wishes to have only the facilitator present. A maximum number of five colleagues and a facilitator is recommended.

▦ The Model

The facilitator schedules the time for the autopsy and arranges for the meeting to be held in a room that is comfortable and confidential. The autopsy should not be held in the treating professional's own office. The autopsy should be uninterrupted with enough time reserved so that the professional does not feel rushed. Allot two hours for the full process of the autopsy. Some autopsies may conclude in a much shorter time; however, a second session may be required at times.

The past supervisor, colleague, or mentor who is conducting the autopsy should begin with housekeeping reminders for the group. This sets the tone for the meeting and provides boundaries and clarity for the group. The facilitator reminds the group that they have two hours for the psychological autopsy. Additionally, the facilitator requests that the meeting be uninterrupted and that all disclosures at the meeting be kept in confidence. Cell phones should be turned off and bathroom breaks kept to a minimum.

The facilitator should describe the nature of the meeting to the group even if everyone believes they understand its purpose. A brief description of the psychological autopsy for the provider is a clarifying reminder that the meeting is for the prime benefit of the recovering professional. For this description of psychological autopsy, the facilitator may state that the meeting being held is for the support and benefit of the treating clinician and that it is voluntary and confidential. The facilitator should state overtly that this autopsy is not a legal procedure or medical investigation. No notes should be taken by anyone in the group.

The facilitator next clearly states the goals of the psychological autopsy. These goals are threefold and include a case review by the surviving professional, expression of thoughts and feelings regarding the suicide, and a review of coping skills and resources for the survivor.

Phase One: The Case Review

The first goal of the psychological autopsy is for the surviving professional to provide a case review. This case review provides an opportunity for the professional to talk about the case in whatever manner or depth he desires. This first step of the autopsy is a cognitive process that allows the professional to think about his work with the patient and attempt to make some sense of the suicide for himself. The structure of this review is determined by the surviving professional so that it will be the most helpful to him. Some professionals may want to review the case in a traditional fashion by describing history and course of treatment. Other professionals may want to describe what they believe are the facts that led to the patient's suicide. Some surviving professionals may have questions to ask of the group; they may wonder whether others would have done anything differently in the treatment of the patient. The professional may specifically want to focus on the last time that he had contact with the patient and wonder whether he could have done or said anything to stop the suicide. Some professional survivors may want to know whether their colleagues would have done things differently; others simply may want to be heard. Some professionals may need to talk about the patient and the experience of being in a therapeutic relationship with that person. In this psychological autopsy, there is no set formula for the case review, and it is a time for the treating clinician to talk frankly about the case and ask questions that may be helpful to him.

In the case review, the professional has the opportunity to look more deeply at the case with his colleagues and process his work. This forum for sharing the case can help the professional see the course of his treatment more clearly, and the feedback from others can be helpful and validating. Although it is not possible for any professional to truly predict the future behavior of any patient, the guilt experienced by the caregiver following a patient suicide can often be overwhelming. The case review may decrease the professional's feelings of guilt as he is reminded by his colleagues that further actions of another cannot be predicted. The action of presenting a case postmortem can be profound for the professional. He may recall moments in the treatment that were warm and loving, meetings that were contentious, or therapeutic mistakes that he believes he made. To have compassionate others be witness to this process in a nonjudgmental fashion can be healing. All the other professionals in the room know that a patient suicide could happen to them, and this somber camaraderie decreases the isolation the surviving professional experiences.

Phase Two: Expression of Thoughts

The opportunity to express feelings regarding the loss of the patient, which is the second goal of the autopsy, may naturally emerge during the case presentation. This part of the process moves the autopsy from the purely cognitive case review to the underlying emotions that may be seething for the professional. The role of the facilitator in helping the professional and the group to navigate this part of the process is critical; the facilitator needs to follow the professional's lead and set the stage for compassion, honesty, and clarity. The case review will likely dovetail with the emergence of feelings; therefore, the facilitator does not need to make any direct statement about moving from the first phase, which is the case review, to the second phase, which is the opportunity to express feelings. These two phases often occur simultaneously.

The facilitator must be aware of the multitude of emotions that the provider may be feeling. The surviving professional may be experiencing deep shame, feelings of failure, vulnerability, fear, and, potentially, depression. She may be having difficulty sleeping and concentrating; she may be finding that she is hypervigilant with other patients and overreacting to signs of depression with others on her caseload. Following the death of a patient by suicide, some professionals may find that they are self-medicating with alcohol, other substances, or prescription medications. During this second phase of the autopsy when emotions may be shared, the professional may disclose that she has been questioning her career. Deeper feelings can emerge with questions about the meanings of life and death. Conversely, some professionals may remain in the cognitive arena and stay far from the disclosure of personal feelings. This may be a personal style and must be respected by the facilitator and the group.

The autopsy may be the first time that the professional has openly presented his case. It is especially important that the facilitator recognize how vulnerable the professional may feel and intervene if others ask questions that are intrusive or inappropriate. If this happens, the facilitator can provide the group with gentle interventions by reminding the group that it is the professional's case review and that it is important to listen rather than make queries. That is not to say that others should not share their personal experiences and feelings. In fact, other professionals participating in the autopsy who share their own stories of loss can be particularly helpful to the surviving professional. The survivor will come to learn that he is not so alone.

Other members of the group and the facilitator himself may find that they are experiencing feelings as their own patient and personal losses resurface. The kind of profound loss such as a patient death by suicide can ripple though a professional community and certainly will affect the psychological autopsy group. Some professionals may become aware that it just as easily could have been their own patient who committed suicide or wonder who on their caseload is at high risk for suicide. Some members may have had a friend or family member commit suicide, and they also will be affected by this event. Other group members may be reminded of different kinds of personal losses and experience feelings reactive to those. The many feelings that may arise in a psychological autopsy can generate not only from the surviving professional, but also from others in the group who have experienced loss.

Everyone participating in the psychological autopsy needs to have the opportunity to talk about themselves as their feelings arise. While it will be helpful for the participant in the autopsy to express his feelings, it is also healing for the surviving professional to hear others' related stories. Nothing is more therapeutic for the provider than to hear that others may have experienced a patient loss themselves and to hear some of the same raging emotions. In a national survey Claude Chemtob noted that 51 percent of responding psychiatrists had a patient who committed suicide.[14] While there may or may not be another provider in the autopsy who has experienced a patient suicide, there will certainly be those who have feared that it could happen to them, or who have had some other sort of traumatic loss. Depending on the developmental stage of each participant, the experiences and reactions may vary. For example, if a young clinician is the surviving professional, or is simply a part of the autopsy, he may find himself wondering just what he is doing in this field. Older, seasoned professionals may have their own set of worries, which can include the fear that their reputation could be ruined by a patient suicide or life review concerns about their entire professional identity as a caregiver. A participant in the autopsy who has experienced a patient suicide in the past may feel re-traumatized; conversely, this person may have worked through the suicide and be able to share thoughts and feelings that can be especially helpful to the surviving professional.

The surviving professional may express a depth of emotion during the autopsy or may be reserved with her feelings. Their process needs to be honored. The group needs to follow the professional's lead and be respectful of how much she wants to share with the group. It is the facilitator's role to ensure that the surviving professional is not victimized by the group. While group members may not mean to push the professional to disclose feelings, subtle pressure can be exerted that this is the "right" way to move forward and heal. This is not necessarily true for everyone. Some individuals do not need to emote and disclose feelings to obtain eventual closure. Individuals heal in their own ways and in their own time. Feelings emerge when they are ready and should never be forced. The psychological autopsy may be viewed by some as the place where feelings need to surface; however, this is not true. Probing for feelings that are not being expressed can create further pain for the professional. It is the facilitator's role to ensure that the group does not query the professional; instead, the group's role is to listen and be supportive. Others in the group may choose to express their own feelings about similar events in their own careers, and this in itself may be useful and cathartic for the surviving professional. Enough time needs to be taken in this phase for the professional to have the opportunity to express herself fully. Additionally, other members of the group should have the time to be able to talk about feelings from their personal experiences as they arise.

When the facilitator feels the group is ready to move out of the emotional phase, he can present a group synopsis of this phase. For example, the facilitator may report back to the group that there are many emotional responses to a patient suicide. The facilitator can further describe the emotional responses that have been demonstrated in the room and acknowledge the feelings that have been shared. The facilitator should not single out the surviving professional's responses; he should use this synopsis to notice the universal feelings that emerge from loss and help normalize the survivor's emotions.

The facilitator's group process skills are needed to determine when the group is ready to move from the first stage of the case review phase and accompanying feelings of the second phase into the third and final phase. The facilitator uses her knowledge and experience to move the group from phase to phase, based on the readiness of the members to proceed. Members may move back into an earlier phase at any time in the process, and feelings can certainly erupt at any time during the autopsy. The phases are meant as a guide for the structure of the autopsy; however, it is crucial to end the autopsy during a cognitive phase and not when emotions are raw. Therefore, the goal for the last phase of the autopsy is to move the group from the emotional to the cognitive as coping skills and recovery are discussed.

Phase Three: Review of Coping Skills

The psychological autopsy began with the cognitive frame of the case review by the surviving professional, moved into feelings from group members, and is ending with a circle back to group cognitions. This model is similar to many crisis debriefing models in that it is designed to ensure that participants are left with cognitive skills to take with them and use in their recovery from the traumatic event, in this case, the suicide. Ending any healing exercise with emotions that are raw may not be beneficial to the participants and, in some cases, could be destructive. Participants will not leave the autopsy with all their feelings tucked neatly into place, but the final phase of this autopsy can provide a container for these feelings and the skills to manage them.

This final phase of the autopsy is one in which a conversation is initiated about coping skills, recovery, and resources. The facilitator will use her skills to best determine when to begin the discussion about recovery, support, and self-care. Once the facilitator decides to move forward with the autopsy, she can begin the third phase by stating that the autopsy is moving into the final phase, which will be a discussion regarding coping strategies and resources. The facilitator may ask the surviving professional if she would like to describe some of the symptoms she has experienced and questions she has about how to handle upcoming events (such as the funeral or contact with the family). If the professional has already discussed symptoms or concerns in a previous phase, the facilitator can review these and ask whether she has others to add that she would like the group to address.

The surviving professional may be experiencing a variety of symptoms in response to the suicide of his patient. The final phase of the psychological autopsy is designed to assist the professional in fortifying and building new strategies and resources to manage these symptoms as they arise. Depending on when the suicide occurred, the professional may have endured many of the initial reactions of the survivor. The coping skills discussed in the third phase of the autopsy may address earlier responses but can also be helpful in managing current and future reactions to the suicide.

The professionals who are present at a psychological autopsy most likely will be well versed in the use of coping skills. It is probable that they have coached many of their own patients in the use of self-soothing techniques and stress-management strategies as part of any treatment plan. It will be important for the group to remember that although the surviving professional may also be knowledgeable in the use of recovery tools for her patients, it becomes a very different matter when the pain is personal. Under trauma, the caregiver may find that all the knowledge and skills that she has to help others are forgotten.

Imagine that first moment when the professional hears that he has lost a patient to suicide. There may be shock, disbelief, and horror. Concentration is likely to be disturbed, if not broken. Preoccupation with the case begins, and the last moments with the patient replayed. Anxiety heightens, and blood pressure may rise. The professional most likely is not reminding himself to take a moment and breathe deeply. Rather, he more likely is racing to pull out the case file and review his notes for clues to the suicide that he may have missed. He may shut his door tightly and isolate himself until his next appointment arrives. During this next session, the professional may not be able to clearly hear or even see the patient in front of him as intrusive thoughts about the deceased patient push their way into the present moment. All of the coping techniques that the professional knows as second nature are lost in the chaos of the trauma. Later, as the shock begins to wear off, new assaults of thoughts and emotions lay siege. Self-doubt, guilt, fear, and vulnerability may set in. The professional may not be able to sleep, and eating can be disrupted. He may begin to drink more alcohol or use drugs to self-medicate or use prescription medication to take the edge off of his anxiety. Some prescription medication may be helpful during the initial stage of recovery; however, if a dependency on this medication develops, it may begin to interfere with daily life.

The professional may develop depression as she wonders about her career and her value as a caregiver. Personal relationships can be affected, and questions about life and its meaning may surface. In some cases, the professional may experience her own thoughts of suicide. While the professional may know exactly how to work with someone else who presented with the same symptoms, she may be paralyzed in helping herself.

In the third phase of the psychological autopsy, the professional has the opportunity to talk about some of the specific symptoms and responses he has experienced in reaction to the suicide. The facilitator can begin the conversation in this phase by asking the professional whether he would like to answer the basic question of how the suicide has affected him. Many of the professional's responses may have been discussed in an earlier part of the autopsy, and if so, the facilitator can name the reactions that have been identified by the surviving professional. For example, the facilitator may report that the group has talked about specific issues such as depression, anxiety, guilt, and fear. It may be useful for the facilitator to note that although everyone in the room certainly has an understanding of coping strategies, during extreme personal stress this knowledge can become cloudy. The facilitator can follow these comments with a query of the group as to methods they have used to manage distress. Other group members can share their collective wisdom from their own losses to assist the surviving professional. The discussion and information provided may be specific to the surviving professional's needs; however, it is the skill of the facilitator that will keep this discussion on track. For example, if the professional speaks about having feelings of depression and lethargy, the facilitator may need to redirect the group if they get off track regarding the recovery skills for this set of specific symptoms.

The group may provide anecdotal stories from their own lives that demonstrate how they have recovered from traumatic events. They may have recovery resources to share with the professional or specific strategies that they use to move through distress. The group may be skilled and aware enough to speak for themselves and not make "you should" statements to the survivor; however, if this is not the case, the facilitator should intervene. A gentle reminder to group members to use "I" statements and speak from their own experience should redirect the wayward member.

The use of cognitive self-talk to stop intrusive thoughts may be discussed as a coping skill. The group members can offer examples of their own experiences that have interfered with their ability to concentrate and explain how they have used thought-stopping techniques to bring themselves back to the moment and away from thoughts about the consuming negative event. Following a patient suicide, the professional may be consumed by thoughts and feelings about the suicide and his role with the patient; as the professional learns to implement thought-stopping techniques, he will be better equipped to manage the other necessary details of life. In the beginning, this self-talk will be difficult, as the survivor may be overwhelmed with emotion and thought. Over time, as the coping skill is implemented and practiced, the intrusive nature of the thoughts can be managed more effectively.

The group may visit other self-soothing reminders, which can include simple techniques, such as reminders to exercise, keep to a daily routine that is well established, eat and sleep at the usual times, and use writing and conversation to express feelings. Although these are familiar details of how to maintain a healthy life when under duress, they can be the parts of one's lifestyle that easily decompensate. Placing a focus back on maintaining daily routine can be a powerful exercise. The professional survivor may not feel like getting out of bed in the morning and may find that she is sleeping later and later. She may not be eating meals because her appetite has diminished significantly. She may be isolating herself, and her use of substances may be on the increase. The group can note that these are some of the behaviors that can occur following a tragedy and share times that these symptoms may have happened with them. The survivor then will not only feel less isolated, but also will gain important reminders to maintain routine. Group members may describe how they managed to keep to a daily schedule and to keep substance use to a minimum. Some group members may have had a positive experience using short-term prescription medications to help with sleep, depression, and concentration. Medication may be helpful for the survivor who experiences extreme weight loss, long-term difficulties with sleep, and feelings of depression. It can be helpful for the professional survivor to hear that her colleagues may have needed medication at one time as well.

It may be useful for the survivor to hear that selecting a set time during the day to grieve and attend to the loss can be helpful. While the feelings and thoughts may emerge at other times during the day, it can be useful for the survivor to have a scheduled time that he can devote exclusively to his grief. For example, setting aside two hours each morning or evening to devote to the grieving process may help the survivor contain the grief that can overtake his daily functioning. The professional survivor can allow himself to go through his daily rituals knowing that he has a period of time set aside in the day to mourn. This is a simple coping strategy that can allow the grief to be acknowledged and still contained.

Group members may share thoughts regarding the use of personal therapy to recover from deep loss. They may have experiences in their own lives when they needed to have important others to talk to and may have experienced deep despair. Using their own stories of recovery and examples of how they coped through these times will decrease the isolation and loneliness of the survivor and provide her with a new skill set for her recovery. The sharing of past traumas and the coping skills used to master them creates an atmosphere of normalcy for the survivor. What she is experiencing is a normal reaction to an abnormal, traumatic event.

The professional survivor may have many concrete concerns about how to deal with the aftermath of the suicide. The group members of the psychological autopsy can be valuable resources for the professional and have objective thoughts and information regarding how some events can best be managed. For example, the group can assist the professional regarding details of dealing with the family members of the deceased, confidentiality, and the law. Group members may not know all the legalese, but they can volunteer to assist the professional in researching questions that may arise that do not have immediate answers.

The professional may fear speaking with their patient's family or friends following a suicide. She may have concerns that the family is enraged at her or that if she speaks with the family, she will face a law-suit. The reality is that most family members of the deceased are ex-traordinarily grateful to the professional if she reaches out to them. The professional cannot share the treatment details of the deceased with the family, but she can listen and share some of her own feelings of loss. Unfortunately, in a world in which litigation is a reality, some families, in their grief, may seek to pursue answers through a lawyer. However, cases of lawsuits against professionals by family members who have had a loved one commit suicide when in treatment are few. The professional must weigh the good that can be done by speaking with a family and sharing sadness against the potential involvement of the law. It is often a frightening question for the professional, and thoughts from other professionals at the autopsy can be illuminating. Speaking with the family of a patient who completed suicide can be one of the most restorative events for the professional when she has the courage to do so.

The professional may also be wondering whether he should attend the funeral of the patient. Questions can arise such as, "How would I introduce myself?" or, "What would I say to others at the funeral?" Some professionals may know that the community has had no idea that their patient was in treatment, while other caregivers may be aware that their patients had disclosed that they were receiving help. The autopsy group can assist the professional in determining whether he should attend the funeral (if desired) as well as how to maintain the confidentiality of the patient, if he does attend. The group may help the professional to see that attending the funeral or even speaking with the family, depending on the circumstances, may not be in the best interest of either the family or the professional. Conversely, the group may support the professional in attending the funeral (if desired by the caregiver) and designate someone to accompany him. The fu-neral may be an emotional event for the professional, and a supportive other should accompany him if he attends.

The autopsy group may recommend that the professional obtain legal counsel. This can be a good resource for the professional to ensure that she does not step into any legal pitfalls surrounding the suicide. An attorney will coach the professional in legal matters per-taining to the death. If there is an ongoing investigation, having an at-torney available to run interference and manage these queries can be helpful and provide a sense of legal safety. The attorney's interference on behalf of the professional can add a sense of legal comfort to the weary caregiver. It can be difficult enough to manage the emotional aftershocks of a patient suicide, but trying to decipher legal matters as well may be especially overwhelming. Additionally, as the professional reviews the case with the attorney who is there to support and represent the professional, a judiciary secondary autopsy is performed. The attorney may not be skilled in helping the professional navigate the emotional and behavioral responses that she has to the death, but he will provide advice and direction on how to proceed legally.

The facilitator should recognize that as the autopsy group members talk about specific events, such as speaking with the deceased's family, attending the funeral, or obtaining counsel from an attorney, the professional's anxiety may rise. While one of the goals of the third phase is to provide resources to the professional, it is most important to decrease the caregiver's anxiety before the autopsy ends and to leave the professional with coping skills. Therefore, if the facilitator notices that the surviving professional is becoming anxious or appears to be feeling overwhelmed by the discussion, it may be necessary to redirect the group. This can be done with a simple, direct statement by the facilitator such as, "I am noticing that this discussion may be raising anxiety; it may be beneficial to return to a conversation about how to cope when feelings such as fear arise." The group members can then return to strategies that can master overwhelming emotions.

Once the autopsy has been running for close to two hours, the facilitator should begin to make some closing statements. A quick review by the facilitator of resources and coping skills that the group members have discussed will bring the meeting back to the cognitive realm. It is especially important to ask each member of the group what the autopsy was like for him or her, ending with the surviving professional. The facilitator may want to ask the group whether they would be willing to convene again in the future if the surviving professional requests a follow-up session. It may be wise to give the professional time to digest the first meeting before determining whether a second one is necessary. The one-time meeting is often enough to provide the professional with an outlet and strategies to manage the issues that arise in the future. Additionally, the professional has found others she may choose to informally talk with when feeling or behaviors related to the suicide affect her. The autopsy has provided the professional with an opportunity to present the case to a nonjudgmental audience, to express her feelings of loss if she chooses to do so, to hear other professionals talk about their own losses and recovery paths, and to have help designing recovery skills and developing resources.

Without the psychological autopsy that is geared to assist the surviving professional with his recovery from patient suicide, the caregiver may be left to try to manage their patient suicide on his own. The care and compassion that can be shown by colleagues and supervisors in the form of a psychological autopsy following a patient suicide may assist significantly in the caregiver's recovery. The simple action of having the autopsy is a way for colleagues to support the provider so he will not feel so alone. David Ness and Cynthia Pfeffer stated, "With striking unanimity therapists have said that formal and informal consultation with colleagues is one of the most important and helpful actions to take in coping with a patient's suicide."[15] Without such intervention, the provider may experience symptoms and behaviors that affect his personal and professional life for years to come.

This practice of the psychological autopsy is designed to provide a compassionate framework in which the provider can join with supportive colleagues to begin to make meaning of what appears to be a meaningless act. The autopsy is the beginning of a process of recovery that will linger in varying states for different caregivers. It is imperative that the professional heal from the loss of her patient suicide if she is to function effectively in the medical or mental health profession. The psychological autopsy that is focused on the professional's recovery is a tool that can augment healing as it leads the professional to greater understanding of herself, others, and her patients. The opportunity to share her fears and self-doubts with others in the same profession helps the caregiver to move to acceptance of herself and reduce self-doubt and blame.

7 ▪ ▪ ▪

Finding Meaning:
Life after Death

People may choose suicide for many reasons. In some instances, their psychic pain may be too much to bear and they just want the feelings of sadness, hopelessness, or anger to stop. In other situations, the individual may be experiencing extreme or chronic physical pain that they decide they can no longer tolerate. One may commit suicide in an impulsive act of retribution against another, believing that the other will suffer from the death. Suicide can be a result of loneliness, humiliation, despair, or physical pain. The choice to kill oneself may be well thought out or could be a spontaneous reaction to an external event.

Life after the death of a loved one to suicide can be painful and tumultuous. The survivor may not have a clear understanding of the meaning behind the loved one's death and may struggle to make her own meaning of the suicide. The survivor will also have to find new meaning for her own existence without her family member, friend, or colleague.

This chapter will explore the controversy regarding self-determination and the right to commit suicide. Letters and notes from those who have killed themselves are included to provide insight into the last days or moments before suicide. The sampling of the letters provided in this document may shed clarity regarding why some felt they needed to end their own lives. These letters may create a way to assist survivors in accepting and making meaning of their profound loss. While these letters are only a representation of final messages, they can provide clues for all suicides. The themes of hopelessness, anger, impulsivity, retribution, pain, and despair are clear. These suicide notes may provide glimpses of how the suicidal individual was feeling and how hard it was for them to go on in the world. The survivor may see that his family member, friend, or colleague chose the path that was best for that person. He may be able to find some peace reflected in the words of others who have also chosen to die by their own hand.

▧ Final Words

Many of the following suicide notes and excerpts have been taken from anonymous sources on suicide, and the note writer's identification has been altered in this book to further protect the identity of the writer. The suicide notes and excerpts from famous people are widely posted with their identifying names; therefore, their sources are noted in this work as well.[1] Some of the final words that will be found on these pages are filled with sorrow. Others are angry. Many are clear that they have thought about their decision and they do not want to go on living in this world. While it may seem impossible to some readers that another human being is so ready to give up his life, try to read the words from the perspective of the suicidal person.

Some people who complete suicide do not leave a note or any clue to their reason for wanting death. The lack of note may in itself be a clue as to the suicidal person's state of mind. Perhaps the pain or lethargy was so great that the person could not bring herself to put her actions into words. Whether or not written words are left behind from the person who has killed herself, the impact of her death will make its mark on those who survive her. The struggle for meaning may be great for the survivor. Perhaps reading the words of others who have taken their own lives will help the survivor to find this meaning.

Famous Suicide Notes

I must end it. There's no hope left. I'll be at peace. No one had anything to do with this. My decision totally.
                                —Freddie Prinze, comedian. Suicide: January 29, 1977.

I feel certain I am going mad again. I feel we can't go thru another of those terrible times. And I shan't recover this time. I begin to hear voices.
                                —Virginia Woolf, author. Suicide: March 28, 1941.

Dear World, I am leaving you because I am bored. I feel I have lived long enough. I am leaving you with your worries in this sweet cesspool—good luck.

     —George Sanders, British actor. Suicide: April 25, 1972.

Frances and Courtney, I'll be at your altar. Please keep going, Courtney, for Frances for her life will be so much happier without me. I LOVE YOU. I LOVE YOU.

     —Kurt Cobain, musician. Suicide: April 8, 1994.

When I am dead, and over me bright April
Shakes out her rain drenched hair,
Tho you should lean above me broken hearted,
I shall not care.
For I shall have peace.
As leafey trees are peaceful
When rain bends down the bough.
And I shall be more silent and cold hearted
Than you are now.

     —Sara Teasdale, poet. Suicide note to her lover who left her.
               Suicide: 1933.

And so I leave this world, where the heart must either break or turn to lead.

     —Nicolas-Sebastien Chamfort, French writer. Suicide: 1794.

With the event of unavoidable and imminent death, it is the simplest of human rights to choose a quick and easy death in place of a slow and horrible one.

     —Charlotte Perkins Gilman, writer. Advocate for the right to die,
       choosing chloroform over cancer. Suicide: August 17, 1935.

The future is just old age and illness and pain.... I must have peace and this is the only way.

     —James Whale, film director. Suicide: May 29, 1957.

I don't believe people should take their own lives without a deep and thoughtful reflection over a considerable period of time.

     —Wendy O'Williams, punk rocker. Suicide: April 1998.

To my friends: My work is done. Why wait?

     —George Eastman, founder of Kodak. Suicide: March 14, 1932.

My wife and I chose to die in order to escape the shame of overthrow or capitulation. It is our wish for our bodies to be cremated

immediately on the place where I have performed the greater part of my daily work during twelve years of service to my people.
> —Adolf Hitler. Suicide: April 30, 1945.

And now, in keeping with Channel 40's policy of always bringing you the latest in blood and guts, in living color, you're about to see another first—an attempted suicide.
> —Chris Hubbock, newscaster. Shot herself during broadcast: 1970.

They tried to get me—I got them first.
> —Vachel Lindsay, poet. Suicide by drinking Lysol: 1931.

To Harald, may God forgive you and forgive me too but I prefer to take my life away and our baby's before I bring him with shame or killing him, Lupe.
> —Lupe Velez, actress. Suicide: December 1944.

All fled—all done, so lift me on the pyre; The feast is over, and the lamps expire.
> —Robert E. Howard, writer. Suicide: June 1936.

Goodbye, everybody.
> —Hart Crane, poet. Last words as he jumped off a cruise ship. Suicide: 1932.

Football Season Is Over. No More Games. No More Walking. No More Fun. No more Swimming. 67. That is 17 years past 50. 17 more years than I needed or wanted. Boring. I am always bitchy. No Fun for anybody. You are getting Greedy. Act your old age. Relax this won't hurt.
> —Hunter Thompson, author. Note left for his wife after weeks of pain from several physical problems including a hip replacement and broken leg. Suicide: February 2005.

Goodbye, my friend, goodbye.
My love, you are in my heart.
It was preordained that we should part
And be reunited by and by.
Goodbye: no handshakes to endure.
Lets have no sadness—furrowed brow.
There's nothing new in dying now
Though living is no newer.
> —Sergei Esenin, Russian poet. Written in his own blood and given to a friend the day before he hanged himself. Suicide: December 1925.

Anonymous Suicide Notes and Letters

I just need this to be over. I've tried to be good and go on but I'm tired. I'm sorry for my children. You will be better off without a crazy-mixed-up mother. You are great kids, this is something in me. You deserve better. I can't live without you and I know you will just get mixed-up with me. Sorry, mom.

My name is Thomas and I have come to the end of my life. The burden of life itself is just too much to take anymore. The last year has been like a black hole sucking me inward, downward into nothingness. It seems as if there is no end to my suffering I know of only one way to put a stop to all of this. I am just a burden to everyone and the world. What does it matter if there is one less human on this over-crowded dirty evil world. We'll all be out of here soon the way humans are going I'm just checking out early. Mom don't think I did this because of something you did or did not do, it's not. I can't control all these emotions I have inside. I've always been a chicken so taking the easy way out is my style. Dad, I know you never loved me and hated me for being born so spit on my grave that should make you happy, huh? So long and goodbye I'm out of here. See you in other worlds. Thomas.

I want to be able to tell someone. I know if I discuss it with anyone ahead of time they will try to stop me. Furthermore, if people knew afterwards, they would feel badly. It is enough for them to grieve me. I don't want them to feel guilty too. It's no one's fault. I have been depressed to the point of suicide before; however, there was always hope. Circumstances today are different—there is no real hope, life would just be long and painful so there's no point. Having decided, I can't talk to anyone about it. Hence this anonymous account. I am researching methods that will not be apparent—I don't want anyone I love to suffer the double loss of knowing it was a suicide. I hope to find something painless, but the more important point is not to cause any more pain than I must. I just want someone to know. I just want someone to know, even though you don't know who I am, that it was really terrible. I have lived many decades trying to do the right thing, and suffering. The pain must just end now. I can't keep taking care of everyone else and never have anything for me. I want to … I want to pour my heart out. But I can't be specific, someone I know may see this. It just hurts so badly, and knowing this time that there really isn't any hope. I have to go. I can't fix anything, I can't change any-thing, and I love so much, and my heart is broken into itsy bitsy pieces. I'm sorry I couldn't be strong anymore. I don't believe in God and and I won't leave a note to torment those I love, but wish

SOMEONE to please forgive me. I'm so sorry. I tried. I really did. That's all I want for my epitaph . . . she tried her very best. I'm so sorry. Goodbye.

I'm sorry that I hurt you with what I did, I didn't mean it. But I can't stand the pain, not any more days. I love him so much and now its over. He left nothing but memories, each one as heavy as tons. Every little thing reminds me of him. The radio plays his favorite song. The world is full of him but my own world is empty now. He kissed another girl and told me it's over and didn't even hear my heart breaking. He said he still loves me but doesn't stand to be with me anymore. Its my own fault. He was all I wanted and now he's gone, gone, gone. And my world is gray and cold and my life is full of tears. And my heart hurts physically when I think of him, and my mind is strong and tells me to end it anyway. I know it . . . But . . . it hurts so deep down inside. How can it hurt so much? And I just wish for a little time without feelings, just a little time without this pain and this hurt that caused my wish to die. Declare it as an accident because my eyes were too drowned with tears to see what I did. Declare it a coincidence because my mind was too occupied with thoughts to realize what I did. Declare it as a murder because he was the one who broke my heart apart. The most painful death can't be as hurting as life without you, my darling. I'll never forget you, never ever. Goodbye cruel world, goodbye cruel destiny. You won. I hope you're satisfied now. Thanks, yours, Sue.

To Janie/Mattie . . .
I have done it too many times I find a girl so special then I f—ed it up because I do or say to them that I have had it NO MORE. I have put these two girls through hell I am worthless NO ONE deserves someone like me in their lives I have never done anything right in my entire life I have thought about this for several months and I have come to a point where I will never be able to be who I want to be so f—k it. I already quit my job and got rid of everything I own (charity I guess was one nice thing I have done in my life). I love Janie so much all I can say here is I am sorry for wrecking your life Janie I really am. Please whoever gets this could you write to Janie and say what I wrote today I just don't have the courage to. Please write her at xxxxxx_xxxxx.com Thanks I AM SOOOOOO SORRY FOR COMING INTO YOUR LIFE AND DOING WHAT I DID WISH YOU COULD HAVE FORGAVE ME MY STUPIDNESS AND BECAME MY FRIEND I LOVE YOU JANIE I REALLY F—ED UP SORRY

From Lisa
Date: Mon, 4 May 2000
I have thought about doing this many times in the past. I have even tried. Some of the times my heart was just not in it. Other times I just did not

succeed. This time I have. No more pills or razor blades. I am going out in style. A single gun shot to the heart. In the parking lot of the funeral home. At least they will not have to go so far to get me. I am so generous! I am sure you are wondering why I did it. Well, let me tell you. My life has been f—ed for a good while now. I have everything most people want. Loving parents, a beautiful baby girl, a wonderful boyfriend, a caring family, a few great friends, lots of acquaintances. The American dream. Yeah, right. Let us stop a minute and laugh at that lie! I am depressed. A lot of people know that already. It's a chemical imbalance. I have a nervous tick that many people may not notice. I have been raped. My mom has breast cancer. My wonderful boyfriend cheats on me. I never graduated from high school. I have no job and live off welfare. I have no future to give my son. Mom and Dad, please do not blame yourselves. It was nothing that you did or did not do. You were always the greatest parents. I could not have asked for a better mom or dad. Please do not mourn my death too much. Shed a tear. Maybe two. Then, go on about your lives. Take care of my baby boy. Never let him forget me. I love you all. May God be with you. To the other people that loved and cared about me. Thank you. You were all wonderful. I love you all. I will never forget you. Keep me in your hearts. To the people that caused me pain and heartache. You know who you are. The message is simple. Choke on your daddy's d— while you burn in Hell. Got that Mother F—ers?? With all my love, Lisa.

I plan to kill myself. My girlfriend was molested and told her mother about what her father did to her after she broke up with me because I couldn't have lived without her and now she won't talk to me. Her mother has banned me from seeing her and they think I'm lying. But I have proof now. I'm going to copy the tapes I tapped my phone and send them to everyone and then I am going to kill myself. I'm not sure how I will do it yet but I think I am going to swallow a lot . . . a lot of medication. Everyone in the world can go to hell now. When I die I hope it hurts them all. I hope they all see what they have done. . . . For once, I will win and no one can beat me.

To Whom It May Concern: The hate that rages within me, rages not for those I love so dearly or those who have crossed my path. The hate rages full force towards me and only me. I have long forgotten those who've hurt me, but I have not and cannot come to terms to forgive myself for the things I have done to myself, and the things I've done to hurt those in my life. You have all touched my life in one way or another, especially those whom I call family. I cannot tell you how sorry I am for ending my life the way I did. I hope you can all find it in your heart to see it as a way for me not to suffer anymore and that I am finally at rest with myself, for being at rest with the guilt that constantly ate at me for so long. Please forgive me for taking my own life so early. I tried so hard to fight against this strong battle. I have reached out for help so many times, and yet I believe I was turned away because of the things I did. That is a punishment I am willing to take, for I know that being who I am has only brought myself and others pain. I love you all and will forever live with the memories we created. Forgive me. Love always and forever, Christy.

I hope this time is it, as I have tried before without much success. Tonight I've been drinking a lot and have 40 valiums and some heroin which I've taken moments ago. Also I have 13 xanax—and I hear xanax and heroin alone can be a lethal combination. I just hope I don't end up in the hospital again, that's agony enough. I'm a peaceful person and hope to leave in my sleep, rather than spat my brains all over with a gun to my head. I don't know what really brings this on, partly the psychosis and the fact that I'm just tired of being f—ed on all the time. Ironically, when I'm nice, warm and caring it seems I get f—ed on even worse. I know everybody knows I have mental problems, and thanks to the few people who have really cared, however I can't be everybody's outcast/scapegoat anymore, and to the people who treated me as such—well, find a new sucker, but be careful because the next one may be more homicidal than suicidal. In the end, I have only myself to blame for being so naive, and I have done some soul searching to really forgive the people who hurt me the most, so I can leave with no animosity toward my fellow human beings. I'm getting sleepy now and keep nodding off from the heroin . . . I'll take the rest now and just say bye (I hope).

Please say goodbye for me to everyone. I guess I just don't fit in and I'm so tired of trying to find a place to belong. Nobody ever wanted me anyway, and I guess nobody ever will and I can't take the pain of the loneliness anymore. I just hope my family can cope without guilt, it's not their fault, it's my self pity, selfishness and self preservation that I can't live with anymore. I wish so badly that I could love and care for another person, but in the alternative for me that's so scary for me to reach out and just say "help me"—so many opportunities to do so, yet I can't, so what's the use of dreaming about it anymore when my fear of rejection has prohibited me from saying three little words: I love you—not in my vocabulary. Things would be so much different if I could open my heart and let people in, but it's not going to happen. Most people gave up much too soon to allow me to care, a vicious cycle that can't go on any longer. So, bye and that's it.

■ Choosing to Die

Does someone have the right to take his own life? Is it a rational choice? Why is societal judgment so harsh and unforgiving when an individual has decided that it is her time to die?

It appears that some distinction in societal values toward suicide is dependent on the circumstances of the self-inflicted death. For example, suicide seems to be more accepted by the survivor and general public when the individual has experienced extreme physical pain or a lengthy illness. Compassion and understanding are more readily available, and positive meaning can be attributed to the loss by survivors when a suicide is the result of a choice to stop physical suffering. The survivor of this type of suicide has been witness to the bodily suffering of the loved one and experiences a sense of meaning and closure once the pain has stopped through death. There is peacefulness to these endings that may not accompany other suicides. The person who has decided to take his own life because of physical distress may have spoken of his choice to die to end his suffering. He may have been able to say his goodbyes and gather support around him at his final moments without fear of being stopped from the act of self-destruction. The decision to die may have occurred in collaboration with loved ones, and, although there will be great grief, there can also be a sense of deep understanding and love that helps the passing to be compassionate and gentle. If someone is able to choose the circumstances of his death, such as time, place, and the people most significant to surround him, then he has created his own meaning regarding his death. All the people invited into the circle of ending will also have had time to create their own meaning of life and death for the suicide of their loved one. This forethought and preparation can help to make the suicide understood and accepted. While the loss will still require a healing process, the recovery will have begun well before the actual suicide.

Imagine the young woman who has late-stage cancer and has been suffering with chronic pain from bone marrow transplants and blood transfusions. Her prognosis is death, and there is no chance for recovery as the cancer is eating away at her major organs. She is in constant, severe pain that cannot be blunted by medication. Her husband and parents are watching her slowly wither away. She is quite conscious and able to make rational decisions. She wants the pain to stop and can clearly say that she is ready to die. Her doctors cannot legally help her to do this, but they can choose to look the other way. She makes a plan with her husband and parents to die at her own home, at her chosen time, surrounded by the people she loves most. She has written her own eulogy and has made videotapes for her husband and parents to watch after her death when they need comforting. She has decided to commit suicide and has spoken about this decision with her family. They have the opportunity to grieve together, to share last moments as they wish, and to make her final wishes an event filled with meaning for all of them. Her death may not be noted as a suicide in the physician's chart because she was going to die. There is a sense of love, acceptance, and peace surrounding her suicide.

Other acts of suicide may not be so accepted and most often do not include the presence of loved ones. There is a discrepancy in our society between physical and mental pain. Stronger validation, sympathy, and credence are afforded to those who can visually show a physical hurt, such as a broken leg or other concrete evidence of suffering. Cards pour in for the physically ill; visitors come and want to know what they can do to help. Hands reach out to support and comfort the physically ill. The mentally ill person, however, is often greeted by others with nervousness, avoidance, and, at times, fear. They do not receive sympathy cards. Instead, others wonder why they just don't do something about their plight. It is a great misunderstanding in our culture that the mentally ill are responsible for their illness and can recover if they would only take action.

Those who suffer from mental illness are often stigmatized, and after the suicide of a mentally ill person, others may believe that the sick person should have been able to "pull themselves out of it." These mentally ill individuals who commit suicide understand that they must do so in secrecy or they will be hospitalized and forced to continue living. The suffering of the mentally ill is often minimized; therefore, the suicidal person may kill himself feeling shame, guilt, or wistfulness. The meaning that he may attribute to his suicide is that, even though he will finally find peace in death from his mental anguish, he leaves others to suffer his loss. Shared meaning about his death is not created with loved ones; therefore, the death is not necessarily peaceful as he may worry about those left behind. Survivors then are left to wonder "why?" and make up their own internal stories about the suicide. Grieving for the mentally ill person may be harder, and understanding regarding why the suicide occurred can be missing or lost. Acceptance becomes a longer process when the person who chooses to die cannot share his intent with his loved ones, yet it may still be too painful for him to go on living. In contrast to the physically ill person who may take his own life with loved ones present who understand and accept his death, the mentally ill person's suicide is generally committed in isolation. This person cannot tell his story of anguish and wish for death. He cannot share his death, or he will be stopped. So he makes a plan in isolation and dies alone. Perhaps he has left a note or a video, trying to explain or comfort his loved ones. He may have come to terms with his own decision for death and have found his own meaning in suicide. However, he dies alone.

The meaning that the mentally ill person places on taking her own life may be complicated by the fact that her illness is misunderstood. While it may be accepted in society for her to ask for help for the illness, it is not acceptable for her to ask for assistance or companionship with her suicide. Yet her suffering may be equal to or greater than that of the person who is physically ill. Imagine, for example, the person who hears voices for most of her life that tell her she is dirty and that the world is a horrible place in which only bad things can happen. Imagine not being able to sleep while the voices drone on and on. Add horrific visions of the devil and hell to voices that may be telling the mentally ill person to harm herself or a loved one. These voices and visions cause an existence that is filled with pain. This is the kind of life some mentally ill individuals struggle with for years. Medication may help, but side effects of the medications can significantly impair life functioning. When these individuals decide to make their final exit, they may experience deep shame for not being able to stay in the world. Our culture condemns them for killing themselves, and the survivor is left with a legacy of shame. The same kind of scenario occurs for the depressed person who has struggled to get out of bed for the last 20 years and finally decides that he does not want to struggle with lethargy and unhappiness anymore. The decision to die is one that must be made alone, or the decision will be halted by others who judge that they are doing what is right in keeping the mentally ill person from suicide.

People choose to kill themselves for many other reasons, as revealed in the suicide notes in this chapter. Some suicides are impulsive, some are made in an act of rage to obtain retribution, and some are well thought out and planned. Judgment is made by others when someone has made the decision to end his own life, and if there is enough warning, interventions will be planned to stop the suicide. Our society struggles with many questions regarding fundamental human rights, yet the decision to take one's own life is seldom considered one of these rights. Eustace Chesser states, "The right to choose one's time and manner of death seems to me unassailable. In my opinion the right to die is the last and greatest human freedom."[2] The debate regarding assisted suicide continues as seen in the imprisonment and subsequent silence of Jack Kevorkian, who was an advocate for assisted suicide in the suffering of the physically ill and dying. Suicide is a question about life and death, choice, freedom, and fundamental human rights. It appears there are no easy answers for some; yet for others, the path is clear.

■ Life after the Death of a Loved One

The assertion that every individual has the personal right to commit suicide is controversial at best. It may be difficult for a survivor of suicide to understand and come to terms with the fact that a loved one made a conscious and deliberate choice to commit suicide. For some of those who chose to commit suicide, the mental or physical anguish that life dealt them propelled them down a path that made death seem the reasonable alternative to prolonged pain. If the survivor can come to terms with this decision, he may be able to feel a greater sense of acceptance of his loss. Finding meaning in a loved one's suicide may be much more difficult for the survivor of suicide than for the person who has committed suicide. The survivor may be caught off guard by the death and not have understood just how much pain his loved one was feeling. Underlying his loss and sadness can be feelings of anger and guilt. There may be a suicide note that will help the survivor to understand, or the note may raise more questions than it answers. When no suicide note is left, the survivor may attribute his own meaning to this lack of communication about the suicide. Throughout the grieving process, the survivor will question his loved one's decision to die. He will struggle to find meaning in the death and in his own life without the family member or friend. The process of letting go is an important one for the survivor. If the survivor can come to terms with the fact that the suicide was a decision made by his loved one, and not an act that he had any choice regarding, it may be easier to heal. To reach these terms of acceptance requires the survivor to find his own life instinct and fortify it. The survivor will need to find meaning in little things each day. He will need to focus on his own resiliencies to move on in the world without his friend or family member, and to find some peace in knowing it was his loved one's decision to die.

8 ■ ■ ■

The Author's Story

■ Who Would Ever Want to Write a Book about Suicide?

When I am asked about my writing, I respond that I am working on a book about suicide. The person asking the question generally appears perplexed, and some people have even offered me their condolences. "That must be depressing" is a comment that I have heard several times over the last few months. People nod when I explain that I am enjoying the project very much but glaze over, quickly change the subject, and certainly don't ask follow up questions. The subject of suicide has been a real conversation stopper.

While it is true that many people think the research and the writing that I am doing must be depressing, it is not. The human psyche is fascinating; delving into the suicidal mind and the aftermath of suicide has been an absorbing journey. It has felt immensely rewarding to put together a book that someone may need to open one day and find the words that will help them to recover from a deep wounding or pain. This person may be experiencing suicidal feelings himself or may be a loved one who is grieving from a loss, or a colleague who is questioning her career because a patient has killed himself.

I have been surprised many times in conversation about my book by others who respond with a story of their personal loss by suicide. I have been struck by just how often my subject matter touches someone personally. In fact, in a few cases I have learned that someone I have known for years was once suicidal herself or has lost a loved one to suicide. All of these individuals who have been touched by suicide have wanted to talk and tell their stories. In some of the dialogues with people about my writing, they have expressed present concerns about a loved one who has appeared depressed. They did not know what to do or how to talk about their concerns, and the subject matter of this book opened a door for them to ask questions. In many instances, I have been able to provide resources and information as a result of a cursory conversation. I have had the opportunity, in the moment, to educate others on how important it is to take suicidal behaviors seriously. So, even before this publishing, I am hopeful that some good has come from this work.

I am a clinical psychologist and a professional survivor of patient suicide. The loss of two patients to suicide has profoundly affected both my professional and personal life. Since the death of my patients, I have wanted to put together a resource recovery guide for other therapists who have experienced the same tragedy; thus, this work was created. Embedded within these book covers is a chapter designed specifically for the recovery of the professional from the loss of a patient to suicide. This chapter began as the heart of this book, and the rest of the writing easily cushioned around it to form a complete work.

I believe that the first sensations of becoming a psychologist began for me when I was in my mother's womb. Seeds for my profession were planted by vibrations and sensations created by the world surrounding my mother. In my early years, I began to master the art of caretaking in a chaotic, loud, and loving Italian family. The imprint of designated family helper became embedded in my personality. Strong beliefs in love and passion were fortified in me by my mother, whose lust for life was encompassing. She taught me to laugh, dance, and sing; to pursue education; and to serve others. My father taught me allegiance and honor and to stand by loved ones with ferocity.

At the age of 14, I fell in love with a boy who also made an imprint in my heart, and the sensation and power of that love will remain with me until the day I die, and with any luck, thereafter. My tenacity in love and life and the depth with which I have always felt connected to others has deepened through the years and formed the basis for my work as a psychologist in the relationships I tend.

My friendships are profound and focused, and attachments are deep and complicated. My life partner provides the one place that is always

my home, wherever we are. Our challenges have deepened our commit-
ment and love; our differences have taught us tolerance and change. I
cannot imagine any world without my husband. He is my perfect
mate—stable, consistent, loving, and beautiful. His love for the planet
and life matches my mother's passion for existence. I am in his debt.

My four stepdaughters organize my love and provide me with purpose. Our oldest, the forest child, is deep, complicated, and rich with
wisdom and compassion. Her existence is colored with warm hues and
the caring for all things, small and large. Our second child, the sun
child, is loving and bright, as beautiful as a sparkling summer day. She
makes me feel admiration and aspire to be better than I am. Our two
little ones are growing like dandelions. I wish I could put rocks on
their heads to stop them from growing, but they reject this concept.
The smallest child is just moving out of the princess phase and into
the rock star attraction, and I can hardly bear it. I miss our princess
but love the soul of this child who is tender and courageous. And, of
course, there is our wild child. She either has her eyes fixed on a movie
or is competing like an Olympian athlete in sports, math, family
games, and life. She faces her challenges with faith, and I am her biggest fan. They are spectacular, resilient children, who teach me every
day about overcoming obstacles and the instinct for life and desire to
be loved.

My patients also form a part of my world, and my love for them is
as unique as any other love. Each of them has touched me in some
way. They have honored me by telling me their stories and sharing
parts of themselves that have been hidden from the outside world. The
reality is that while the psychologist spends only a short hour a week
with her patient, it is a time that is filled with intimacy and meaning.
The therapist-patient relationship is created out of trust and a desire
from one to be healed and the other to assist with the healing. While
this relationship does not physically expand beyond the office walls,
the patient carries the therapist's words and image with him in his
daily routines. The therapist, albeit to a lesser extent, also carries
images of the patient and the work that the two are creating. When a
patient kills himself, the therapist is left to try to make sense of the
suicide and loss.

In my career I have survived the suicide of two of my patients. Their
deaths have had a profound and lasting impact on my life and on my
work. In fact, the ending of their lives was in part the reason for this
book. I continue to try to make meaning of their deaths and create an
internal understanding of why they died and, in doing so, attempt to
find some comfort for myself. I will alter their identifying information
as I tell their stories and how they affected me, and I thank them for

propelling me down the road on a quest for greater purpose and reason.

I was a young master's level clinician and barely wet behind the ears when my first patient killed herself. While young and hopeful, I clearly knew that I was over my head in treating this young woman who was so troubled. My patient was a young adult woman with a history laced with violence; she carried a weapon at all times, sought out dangerous situations in which she could provoke confrontations, and attended therapy only because she was court mandated to do so. She was a prostitute and would sometimes assault her johns. She would saunter into my office with a large knife strapped to her leg and "tease" me by ensuring that the tip of the blade showed under her pant leg. She would sometimes show up intoxicated. At times, she would be verbally abusive to me, and at other times she would be remorseful. During her remorseful sessions, I could see the part of her that wanted help, that sought love and understanding, and that was so hurt by early experiences that she lashed out at the world around her. She had connected with me in her own unique way. However, I knew I was out of my league in trying to treat her. At that point in my career, I did not know how to effectively use my own supervision to talk about cases; conversely, my supervisor did not grasp the fact that I was having such difficulty with this particular patient. My judgment with my patient was clouded by my own anxieties and fears. I had talked with her about the knife and how she could not be allowed in the building with a weapon. She returned during the next session with the weapon, and I confronted her. She denied that the knife was strapped to her leg although it was clearly showing. I decided that I felt too unsafe to continue to see her and discussed a transfer to another therapist. She refused to see anyone else but me. A joint session was scheduled with my patient, myself, and a new therapist to discuss the transfer and say goodbyes, regardless of the patient's wish to continue seeing me. The transfer was made, and my patient began a course of therapy with a new male therapist. I knew she was coming to the clinic and that she worked with this new therapist until her probation was up. Six months later I found out that she had hanged herself in her bedroom.

I sometimes still think I see her. I imagine that I have a brief glimpse of her standing on a corner, or sitting in a restaurant. When I look more closely, the image is gone, or it is only a stranger. I feel guilt, which has lessened over the years but is still present. I wonder if I had been a more seasoned therapist whether I could have made a difference in deepening our connection, thereby saving her life. I attended her funeral, and her mother asked me to visit her several times at her home, which I did. Her mother had a need to show me the room in which her daughter had hanged herself. The noose still haunt-ingly remained attached to the ceiling rafter. My patient's mother did not blame me. She needed me to listen as she expressed her own grief, sadness, and own guilt. I questioned my career. I questioned my ability. I wondered whether everyone was looking at me and thinking that I should have done something more, that I never should have aban-doned my patient.

I did not know how to use my supervision to grieve. I had not yet begun my own personal depth therapy, and I did not feel like I could talk to my colleagues about the suicide of this patient. At the time, the male therapist who last treated my patient seemed to me to have moved through the knowledge of her suicide quickly and without much impact; now I wonder if he suffered more that I was aware. No one talked with me about the suicide; perhaps they feared I would feel worse if they broached the subject. I plodded on in a haze for several weeks and never really processed the loss of this patient formally, even to this day. In writing "my story" in this book, I discovered that the only way I could address the suicide of my patients was to first write about what sustains me, my family and friends.

I went on in my career to earn my doctorate in clinical psychology and to practice psychology both in a private practice and as the direc-tor of several clinics. I work individually with patients, provide supervi-sion and administration, teach, and consult. My work is exciting, rich, and fulfilling.

A few years ago I met with another female patient for a one-time visit. She was clearly distraught over her relationship with her hus-band, who was having an affair. She was having difficulty sleeping and exhibited some of the classic signs of depression. She denied feeling su-icidal or homicidal and stated that she was beginning to feel more hopeful about her situation because she had a date scheduled with her husband over the weekend. We talked about coping skills, and how she would manage her feelings if the date did not go well. She was pro-vided with emergency contact information, and she promised to call the emergency numbers if she felt worse between appointments. At the sessions end she lingered at the door. I was aware of my next patient in the waiting room. She left the office, and the following week I was contacted by the police, who found my business card in her pocket. Over the weekend, she had shot her husband and then shot herself. I experienced many of the feelings that I described in the Chap-ter 6 case example. I felt shock and horror, and, at first, I couldn't believe that it had happened. Following the emotions of shock and dis-belief came the questioning and self-doubt. What more could I have done? How could I have missed the possibility that this could have happened? Why didn't I call the patient back into my office when she lingered in the doorway?

My concentration was disturbed. I became hypervigilant with every other patient. If anyone on my caseload mentioned or gave evidence of slight depression or even sadness, I went overboard in making safety plans and in my questioning. I found it difficult to sleep. I felt guilty all the time and fearful that I would miss other signs of suicide in other patients. In my staff supervision, I also became unduly hypervigilant regarding the treatment of my staff's patients.

As a seasoned psychologist, I felt great shame that I lost a patient to suicide and, additionally, felt the burden of her husband's murder. I had only seen this patient one time, and the depth of a long-term relationship had not been formed; however, the impact of the homicide-suicide was still profound, and my functioning as a psychologist was affected. Additionally, my personal relationships suffered as I tried to come to terms with the deaths. I knew that I needed to do something to salvage my work with other patients before I caused harm by overreacting. I tried to talk about the suicide with my colleagues, but they seemed to distance themselves from the conversation. I believe each had their own set of fears regarding suicide and also had concerns that if they talked about my patient's suicide-homicide, I would feel worse. No one asked me about my feelings. I felt lost in a vacuum.

I decided to contact an older mentor with whom I had worked for many years and for whom I had a deep regard and trust. I had an instinctual need to review the case with someone objective, and I asked him to sit with me while I looked at the window of time that I had spend with this patient. He agreed, and I traveled out of state to meet with him. My mentor was a wizened psychiatrist, seasoned from years of working with disturbed individuals. I had not seen him for many years, and his stature still filled the room. We caught up with each other's lives; he was ready to retire, and I was midcareer. We recalled challenging patients we had shared years ago. It felt easy to rekindle our relationship even after the many years that had passed.

My mentor asked me to talk about my patient. I had the case file with me, but I left it closed on the desk as I reviewed the session that day. I wept as I recalled the moment that my patient had lingered in my doorway and talked about how guilty I felt that I had not asked her to sit back down. I still wish I could change that moment. My mentor had tears in his eyes as he listened. He looked at my notes, written on the day of the session with my patient in which I had documented her denial of suicidal-homicidal feelings and noted a plan to call between sessions if these feelings emerged. He read some of the words back to me. He reminded me that psychologists have no ability to predict the future behaviors of our patients and we can work only with the information that they provide from the questions we ask. His words were soothing.

What helped me the most that day was that my mentor shared a story of his own patient suicide. After a long and fruitful career of working with troubled people and saving many lives, he had experienced his first patient suicide in the last month. He was entering retirement, and I could only imagine what it must have felt like for him to end his career with such a significant loss. It was clear to me that he had not yet shared his story with anyone, and we talked together about our losses and how they affected our professional and personal lives. It was as if we had found each other in this lonesome world of loss and could share thoughts and feelings that no one else could really understand. I will be indebted to him for welcoming me into his world, listening to my story, and sharing his own pain.

This meeting was the first step for me to make some sense and meaning out of the loss of my patient and my own continued work as a psychologist. I continued to grieve and process the suicide-homicide in my own clinical supervision with another wonderful mentor. My patient suicides still periodically need to be addressed in my supervision if I become hypervigilant or retraumatized by a familiar patient story.

Through my own experience I became aware of the limited resources for those working in the mental health and medical fields who are survivors of suicide. The suicide of a patient was clearly a subject that was difficult for my colleagues; and, therefore, the professional survivor is often left to her own devices to recover. There was little available material in the literature when I attempted to find solace in reading about how to cope with my loss. Seeds were planted for this book through my own loss and pain.

It has been several years since the loss of my last patient to suicide. I am all too aware that another of my patients could commit suicide at any time. I am vigilant but try not to be hypervigilant. It is a fine line to walk. I use my experience to talk with both young therapists and more seasoned therapists who have experienced their own patient suicide or fears about patient suicide. The suicide of a patient is a risk that the professional mental health worker consciously decides to take in doing this work. Statistics indicate that one in five mental health providers will experience a patient suicide in her career. I wonder whether these statistics are not much higher.

This book began to form in my mind many years ago. I wanted to design a formal recovery plan for professional survivors of patient suicide. My editor liked the concept but thought the topic too narrow;

thus, this complete work was born. It has been healing for me to write. My scars will never completely heal, but I am not sure that is a bad thing. My experiences have given me the understanding and words to use with others. My experiences keep me on my toes. I do not take any patient word or gesture for granted. I have learned that I cannot control what happens when a patient leaves my office. Nor am I necessarily accountable for a patient's future actions, especially if they provided no clues to intent.

I love my family and friends. I have deep loves that remain with me from years ago. I love my work as a psychologist. I love my patients. My hope is to spread this love in some small way, every day.

9 ▪ ▪ ▪

Conclusion

▪ Case Example: Hope and Recovery

Brian had been hospitalized three times for serious suicide attempts. He was considered to be in the high-risk group for completing suicide because he had many of the factors that can lead to suicide. Brian was fairly isolated with few friends or concerned family members; he was middle age, he had episodes of drinking heavily, and his family history gave evidence of generations of family members suffering from depression. His greatgrandfather had killed himself with a shotgun before Brian was born. Even more worrisome, Brian felt very hopeless and really wanted to die.

During his previous hospitalizations Brian was connected with community supports and resources. He did not follow through with either the connections that were provided to him or with his medication. His depression deepened and by the third hospitalization his therapist began to feel helpless herself in finding ways to help Brian. She decided to make changes in his treatment plan. Although the therapist had recommended Alcoholics Anonymous (AA) in the past, for the first time, she connected Brian with a sponsor from AA while he was still hospitalized.

Brian had some internal resiliencies that had not yet been tapped through his therapy. His AA sponsor made an easy connection with Brian as he reminded Brian of an uncle who used to take him fishing and spend time with him when he was a child. Upon Brian's discharge from the hospital, the sponsor accompanied him to several AA meetings. Brian began to make associations with others who he felt understood him. His sponsor made it a requirement of his involvement with Brian to continue on his medication, and for the first time, Brian began to experience the benefits of the antidepressants. As his depression lessened, Brian's cognitive functioning improved. He was bright, which was another of his resiliencies, and soon began to use some of the cognitive techniques he learned in his therapy to change his negative thinking. The AA meetings that he attended daily also kept him focused on what was positive and significantly decreased his isolation. Brian described feeling like "himself" for the first time he could remember.

With the combination of medication, therapy, and AA, Brian's thoughts of death and dying diminished and over time became a distant memory. If he began to experience thoughts of suicide, Brian now had the energy and desire to reach out for help to his support system. His collaborations at AA strengthened to become friendships and his "family of choice."

When Brian told his story in AA, he sometimes couldn't believe he was the same person he was describing to the group. He talked about his childhood and his alcoholic, depressed father and his mother who worked all the time and never had time for him. He recalled his first drink at the age of 12, how his first years of drinking made him feel better about himself, and how he would forget his loneliness in the alcohol. He remembered how he isolated himself from others and then drank to console himself. Brian described how the alcohol contributed to the state of depression that he had always experienced, and how he wanted to die and end the ongoing cycle of drinking and depression. Every time Brian would get into a relationship, his drinking would become a problem for his partner and he would be left, increasing his wish to die. He described his first suicide attempt by gunshot and how the police broke down his door to rescue him. He recalled not caring whether he lived or died, and being resistant to everything his counselor would suggest to help him recover. When he told his story to the group, he would shake his head with some disbelief. Now that his head was clear from the alcohol and his depression had lifted he could clearly see the toxic cycle he had been caught in. He talked about his inability to reach out and the fact that when someone tried to help him he rejected them.

Brian also told the group about his deep gratefulness. He looked back at the journey of his life and could see that others easily could have given up on him, but did not. He identified his first glimmer of hope in life as the connection he made with his sponsor, who was someone he felt could understand him. His sponsor pushed him to find the resiliencies that were buried and to focus on those, not his deficits. He knew that he had been determined to die and that if he had continued down the road he was headed that he eventually would have completed suicide. While his first hospitalizations or his therapist could not dissuade him off the path to suicide, their attentions bought him the time he needed until he found his path to life.

■ The Truth about Suicide

The first real truth about suicide is that if someone decides that they want to die they eventually will be able to find a way to kill themselves. No other single person has control over another; and while there may be ways to intervene in a suicidal act, there will be other moments and opportunities that the suicide can be completed. If someone has decided to die by their own hand, ultimately this death may not be stopped. Important others do not have the control to stop a loved one's death if they are determined to die. If those who survive suicide can come to understand and accept this, they may begin to find their own path to recovery.

While this truth is real and profound, there are other important truths regarding suicide. There is help for the suicidal person. Causes for suicidal feelings and behaviors may come from early formation of the self or later life events. The good news is that for each cause of suicidal thought, an intervention is available to alter the course of action leading to completed suicide. The key is for the suicidal person to reach out for help or for a concerned other to help propel the individual toward assistance. Once the cause(s) of suicidal thoughts are identified, a treatment plan and resources can be put in place to make changes and improve quality of life. The evidence is in that treatment of depression and suicidality is highly successful with a combination of therapy and medication. This is excellent news; the task remains to propel the person who experiences suicidal tendencies to seek professional assistance. Many internal and external resources can be exposed and tapped into to assist the suicidal person in their healing journey, once they are engaged in professional help. Not all individuals will be willing to begin medication or to engage in therapy. One method of treatment many not be enough to manage the suicidal thoughts. Building outside supports and creating a "team" of involved others to be available to the person who struggles with suicide may be enough to thwart suicidal intent in some individuals. This team of involved others does not necessarily need to be a formal one; it can include support groups such as AA or Alanon, family members, therapy, crisis workers, friends, spiritual groups, and cultural connections. No one alone should be in the position of feeling responsible for the well-being of someone who suffers with depression. If a concerned other finds herself in this position, she should seek professional support for herself.

Another truth about suicide is that there is help for those who survive the loss of a loved one to suicide. When a friend or family member completes suicide, everything changes. The world doesn't seem the same. Others do not understand the profound loss. The grief is huge and incomparable to other losses. Survivors often experience guilt and shame and wonder whether they could have somehow stopped the suicide. Survivors may experience troubling symptoms themselves that can include depression, suicidal thoughts, trouble sleeping and eating, difficulty concentrating, and uncontrollable emotions such as crying or anger and nightmares. The survivor may need professional intervention if the symptoms are prolonged. As with the suicidal person, the key is to reach out for help, because it is waiting and available.

A fourth truth about suicide is that the professional who has worked with someone who completes suicide may be affected both personally and professionally. The professional may experience some of the same symptoms as the family and friend survivors. Additionally, the professional may find herself questioning her career as well as her ability to perform or may even quit her profession. These individuals may be psychologists, therapists, medical doctors, emergency room workers, case managers, or anyone who has a professional relationship with a client. While the assistance available is more limited for the professional, it still exists. It may be useful for the professional to seek personal counseling or speak with a colleague or supervisor regarding feelings that can be overwhelming or affect the treatment of other clients. Unfortunately, no support groups are known to this author for the professional regarding patient suicide and only limited literature is available. This book provides a guide to assist professionals in their own recovery from the death of a patient by suicide.

In almost all cases, suicide is a difficult event to comprehend. This book attempts to shed understanding regarding just how the suicidal mind can develop in the young person and later affect life functioning as an adult. This book offers hope to both the suicidal person and the survivor in the form of recovery strategies and making meaning of suicide. It also wrestles with difficult questions regarding the individual's right to commit suicide. The event of a suicide may never be comprehensible to those who are left behind. However, this book has created a frame within which those who experience suicidal thoughts, or live on following the death of a loved one to suicide, can begin to heal.

Resources

The resources provided on the following pages are intended for anyone who may be feeling depressed or suicidal as well as for the family, friends, and co-workers who have survived a completed suicide. They also are useful for professionals who want to learn more about suicide intervention and for members of the general public who may have an interest in providing donations, research, or learning more about suicide.

American Association for Suicidology
The primary goal of the American Association for Suicidology is to understand and prevent suicide. This association promotes research, public awareness programs, and public education for professionals and volunteers. The association is also notable as a clearinghouse on information regarding suicide.
1-202-237-2280
http://suicidology.org

American Foundation for Suicide Prevention
The American Foundation for Suicide Prevention is dedicated to understanding and preventing suicide through research and education, and

to reaching out to people with mood disorders and people affected by suicide.
1-888-333-AFSP
inquiry@afsp.org
http://www.afsp.org

Centers for Disease Control and Prevention

The mission of the Centers for Disease Control and Prevention (CDC) is to promote health and quality of life by preventing and controlling disease, injury, and disability. This organization has links to many forms of information regarding depression and suicide, including suicide prevention.
1-800-311-3435
1-404-498-1515
http://www.cdc.gov

Centre for Suicide Prevention

The Centre for Suicide Prevention is a nonprofit organization with three primary goals. The Centre provides information regarding suicide in a specialized library and resource center. It also provides caregiver training in suicide intervention, awareness, bereavement, crisis management, and related topics. Additionally, the Centre supports research on suicide and suicidal behavior.
1-403-254-3900
http://www.suicideinfo.ca

Compassionate Friends

The Compassionate Friends is a national association designed to assist families in the positive resolution of grief following the death of a child of any age and to provide information that will help others to be supportive.
1-630-990-0010
nationaloffice@compassionatefriends.org
http://www.compassionatefriends.org

Dougy Center

The Dougy Center is a national center that provides resources and support for children and teens who are grieving the death of a parent, sibling, or friend.
1-503-775-5683
http://www.dougy.org

National Institute of Mental Health

The National Institute of Mental Health (NIMH) is a national organization dedicated to research that is focused on the understanding,

treatment, and prevention of mental disorders and the promotion of mental health. Information and links to research regarding suicide statistics and prevention can be found at this Web site.
1-866-615-6464
nimhinfo@nih.gov
http://nimh.nih.gov

National Organization for People of Color against Suicide
The National Organization for People of Color against Suicide (NOPCAS) was formed to address the tragic epidemic of suicide in minority communities. This organization seeks to improve knowledge for professionals, share coping methods, educate bereaved family and friends, share information on suicide prevention and intervention, and provide insight on depression.
1-202-549-6039
info@nopcas.com
http://www.nopcas.com

National Suicide Prevention Hot Line
This National Suicide Prevention Hot Line provides the public with immediate help for anyone who is feeling suicidal or is concerned about a loved one who may be suicidal. The crisis workers are on call 24 hours a day, seven days a week, and will connect the caller with a crisis worker in his area so that he can talk with someone who cares and can receive referrals to community supports as requested. Those who are experiencing suicidal thoughts and feelings can call this number as well as those who may be concerned about a family member, co-worker, or friend. The calls are free and confidential. This is an excellent resource if you are feeling depressed or suicidal. You will be connected with a professional who can help. It is a good resource for concerned others who have questions about how to assist others in getting the help they need This hotline can direct concerned others to help in dealing with their own feelings regarding a suicidal loved one or the completed suicide of a family member, friend, or colleague.
1-800-273-TALK (8255)
http://www.suicidepreventionhotline.org

Office of Minority Health
The Office of Minority Health (OMH) provides information on health issues specific to African Americans, American Indians, Alaska Natives, Asian Americans, Hispanics, Native Hawaiians, and Pacific Islanders. This resource center collects and provides information on a variety of health topics, including substance abuse and depression. The information on this site regarding suicide is limited, however.

1-240-453-2883
info@omhrc.gov
http://www.omhrc.gov

Parents, Families and Friends of Lesbians and Gays
Parents, Families and Friends of Lesbians and Gays (PFLAG) promotes the well-being of gay, lesbian, transgendered, and bisexual persons and represents the families and friends of lesbian, gay, bisexual, and transgendered persons. The information on this Web site may assist these individuals by providing support and connection to those who deal with depression and suicidality that may result from being a member of an underrepresented population.
1-202-467-8180
info@pflag.org
http://community.pflag.org

Stop a Suicide Today
Stop a Suicide Today is a program that provides information on signs of depression and facts about suicide and mental illness. This program also provides information on how to help a friend, links to the National Depression Screening Test, information to find a professional in a particular geographic area, and information for survivors.
1-781-239-0071
http://www.stopasuicide.org

Suicide Prevention Action Network USA
The Suicide Prevention Action Network (SPAN) is dedicated to preventing suicide through public education and awareness, community engagement, and federal, state, and local grassroots advocacy. SPAN seeks to empower those who have been touched by suicide.
1-202-449-3600
http://www.spanusa.org

Suicide Prevention Resource Center
The Suicide Prevention Resource Center provides states, government agencies, private organizations, colleges and universities, and suicide survivor and mental health consumer groups with access to information and experience that support their efforts to develop programs, implement interventions, and promote policies to prevent suicide. A feature of this site is that it provides information for each state in a dropdown menu.
http://www.sprc.org

Suicide Reference Library
The Suicide Reference Library was created by as an outreach project by volunteers and provides information for those who are involved in suicide awareness, grief support, and education activities.
http://www.suicidereferencelibrary.com

Survivors of Suicide
Survivors of Suicide is an independently owned and operated Web site designed to help those who have lost a loved one to suicide. This Web site provides information so that all those who have lost someone to suicide can begin to resolve their grief and pain in their personal manner.
http://www.survivorsofsuicide.com

Notes

Introduction

1. American Foundation for Suicide Prevention, *Surviving a Suicide Loss: A Resource and Healing Guide* (New York: AFSP, 2008).

2. Ibid.

Chapter One

1. Ellenor Mittendorfer-Rutz, Anders Rasmussen, and David Wasserman, "Nurture Versus Nature: Evidence of Intrauterine Effects on Suicidal Behavior," *Lancet* 364 (2004): 1103.

2. Ibid.

3. Donald Winnicott, *Maturational Processes* (New York: Basic Books, 1963).

4. Kristine Bertini, *Marital Status and Midlife: Perceptions of Early Parenting and Perceptions of Self* (Ann Arbor: University of Michigan Press, 1995), 25.

5. Winnicott, *Maturational Processes*.

6. Bertini, *Marital Status,* 26.

7. Sigmund Freud, *Three Essays on the Theory of Sexuality* (London: Imago, 1905).

8. Christopher Tennant, "Parental Loss in Childhood: Its Effect in Adult Life," *Archives of General Psychiatry* 45 (1988): 1045–1050.

9. John Bowlby, *Attachment and Loss* (New York: Basic Books, 1973).

10. Carl Jung, *Man and His Symbols* (New York: Dell Publishing Co., 1964).

11. Barbara M. Richards, "Suicide and Internalized Relationships: A Study from the Perspective of Psychotherapists Working with Suicidal Patients," *British Journal of Guidance and Counseling* 27, no. 1 (1999): 85–98.

12. Heather B. Twomey, Nadine Kaslow, and Shannon Croft, "Childhood Maltreatment, Object Relations and Suicidal Behavior in Women," *Psychoanalytic Psychology* 17, no. 2 (2000): 313–335.

13. John Briere and Marsha Runtz, "Differential Adult Symptomatology Associated with Three Types of Child Abuse Histories," *Child Abuse and Neglect* 14 (1990): 57–64.

14. Thomas Joiner, *Why People Die by Suicide?* (Cambridge, MA: Harvard University Press, 2005).

15. Mac Marshall. *Weekend Warriors: Alcohol in a Micronesian Culture* (Palo Alto, CA: Mayfield Publishing, 1977).

▦ Chapter Two

1. Edwin Shneidman, *The Suicidal Mind* (New York: Oxford University Press, 1996).

2. Roberta Satow, *Gender and Social Life* (Boston: Allyn & Bacon, 2000).

3. Samuel Vaknin, *Malignant Self Love* (Prague: Narcissus Press, 2007).

4. "American Roulette: The Untold Story of Murder-Suicide in the United States" (Washington, DC: Violence Policy Center, 2002).

5. *Guide to Clinical Prevention Services,* 2nd ed. (Washington, DC: United States Preventative Services Task Force, 1996).

▦ Chapter Three

1. Liz Grauerholz, "An Ecological Approach to Understanding Sexual Revictimization: Linking Personal, Interpersonal, and Sociocultural Factors and Processes," *Child Maltreatment* 5 (2000): 5–17.

2. Stevan Hobfoll, *Stress, Culture and Community: The Psychology and Philosophy of Stress* (New York: Plenum Press, 1998).

3. George Bonanno, "Loss, Trauma and Human Resilience: Have We Underestimated the Human Capacity to Thrive under Extremely Adverse Events?" *American Psychologist* 59 (2004): 20–28.

4. Jon A. Shaw, "Les Enfants of Duplessis: Perspectives on Trauma and Resiliency," *Psychiatry* 69, no. 4 (Winter 2006): 328–332.

5. Diane Papalia, Sally Wendos Olds, and Ruth Feldman, *Human Development,* 7th ed. (Boston: McGraw Hill, 1998).

6. Katey Baruth and Jane Carroll, "A Formal Assessment of Resilience: The Baruth Protective Factors Inventory," *Journal of Individual Psychology* 58, no. 3 (2002): 107–117.

7. Jeremiah Schumm, Melissa Phillips, and Stevan Hobfoll, "Cumulative Interpersonal Trauma and Social Support as Risk and Resiliency Factors in Predicting PTSD and Depression among Inner City Women," *Journal of Traumatic Stress* 19 (2006): 825–836.

8. Papalia, *Human Development,* 7th ed.

9. Ibid.

10. Ibid.

11. Michelle Dumont and Marc Provost, "Resilience in Adolescents," *Journal of Youth and Adolescence* 28, no. 3 (1999): 343–363.

12. Phillip Bowman, "Role Strain and Adaptive Issues," *Counseling Psychologist* 34 (2006): 118.

13. Karen Reivich and Andrew Shatte, *The Resilience Factor* (New York: Random House–Doubleday, 2002).

14. Albert Bandura, *Self-Efficacy: The Exercise of Control* (New York: Freeman, 1997).

■ Chapter Six

1. Michael Sacks, Howard Kibel, and A. M. Cohen, "Resident Response to Patient Suicide," *Journal of Psychiatric Education* 11, no. 4 (1978): 217–226.

2. American Foundation for Suicide Prevention, *Surviving a Suicide Loss.*

3. Herbert Hendin, Ann Pollinger Haas, John T. Maltsberger, Katalin Szanto, and Heather Rabinowicz, "Factors Contributing to Therapist's Distress after the Suicide of a Patient," *American Journal of Psychiatry* 161 (2004): 1442–1446.

4. Irving Steingart, *A Thing Apart* (New York: Jason Aronson, Inc., 1995).

5. Richard Summers and Jacques Barber, "Therapeutic Alliance as a Measurable Psychotherapy Skill," *Academic Psychiatry* 27 (2003): 160–165.

6. Tori DeAngelis, "Surviving a Patient's Suicide," *APA Monitor* 32, no. 10 (2001): 70–72.

7. Larry Zaroff, "Cool Heads and Cold Heart," *New York Times,* February 2007.

8. Carl Jung, *Man and His Symbols* (New York: Doubleday, 1969).

9. Kay Jamison and R. J. Baldessarini, "Effects of Medical Interventions on Suicidal Behaviors," *Journal of Clinical Psychiatry* 60 (1999): 4–6.

10. Eric Plankun, "Responding to Clinicians after Loss of a Patient to Suicide," *Psychiatric News* 21 (2005): 10.

11. "Suicide Prevention and Psychological Autopsy," Pamphlet 600-24 (Washington, DC: Department of the Army, 1988).

12. Fred Cutter, "Suggestions for Psychological Autopsy," *Suicide Prevention Triangle* (2005).

13. Edwin Shneidman, "The Management of the Presuicidal, Suicidal, and Postsuicidal Patient," *Annals of Internal Medicine* 75 (1971): 441–458.

14. Claude Chemtob et al., "Patient's Suicides: Frequency and Impact on Psychiatrists," *American Journal of Psychiatry* 145 (1988): 224–228.

15. David Ness and Cynthia Pfeffer, "Sequelae of Bereavement Resulting from Suicide," *American Journal of Psychiatry* 147, no. 3 (1990): 279–285.

■ Chapter Seven

1. All of the notes and excerpts from both famous people and anonymous sources in this section are from the Web site "Brain Candy," http://www.corsinet.com/braincandy/dying3.html.

2. Eustace Chesser, *Why Suicide* (London: Arrow Books, 1999), 123.

Index

About the Author

KRISTINE BERTINI is Clinical Psychologist and Director of the University of Southern Maine Health and Counseling Service. She is Chair of the University Task Force on Suicide Intervention and a member of the Governor's Steering Committee on Suicide Prevention.